MORE GOLD IN YOUR PIANO BENCH

Collectible Sheet Music

Inventions, Wars, and Disasters

MARION SHORT

Schiffer Publishing Ltd
77 Lower Valley Road, Atglen, PA 19310

Photography by Roy Short

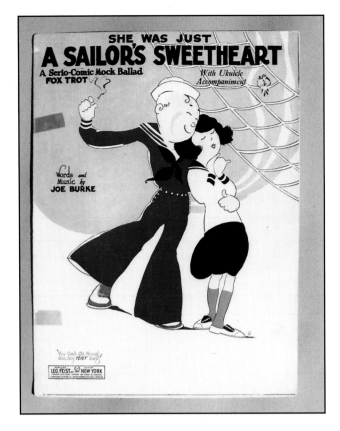

Fair winds and following seas to my favorite sailor...

ISBN: 0-7643-0012-1

Printed in China

Designed by Bonnie Hensley

Library of Congress Cataloging-in-Publication Data

Short, Marion.
    More gold in your piano bench: collectible sheet music: inventions, wars, and disasters/Marion Short; photography by Roy Short.
        p. cm.
    Includes bibliographical references (p.173) and index.
    ISBN 0-7643-0012-1 (paper)
    1. Popular music--United States--History and criticism. 2. Music title pages--Collectors and collecting--United States. 3. Inventions--Songs and music--History and criticism. 4. War songs--History and criticism. 5. Disasters--songs and music--History and criticism. I.Title.
ML3477.S56 1997
781.64'0263'0973--dc21   97-5156
                                                                          CIP
                                                                          MN

Published by Schiffer Publishing, Ltd.
77 Lower Valley Road
Atglen, PA 19310
Phone: (610) 593-1777
Fax: (610) 593-2002
E-mail:schifferbk@aol.com
Please write for a free catalog.
This book may be purchased from the publisher.
Please include $2.95 for shipping.
Try your bookstore first.

We are interested in hearing from
authors with book ideas on related subjects.

Even in its day sheet music was acquired and cherished not only for performance but also for a vague but real "cultural delight." It is easy to disparage a preoccupation with personal property; but it is important, too, to understand that the possession of items of beauty should be seen as serving to elevate the owner, the listener, or the beholder. Historical collections reflect and foster owners who are thereby the more humane, more filled with delight, good taste, and understanding of human history, and thus more responsive to one's fellow citizenry and the democratic society that was part of the collective national vision.

D. W. Krummel
Bibliographical Handbook of American Music
University of Illinois Press, 1988

ACKNOWLEDGMENTS

Many thanks to all who have helped and encouraged me with this book. Advanced collectors from the National Sheet Music Society have been most supportive, in particular James Nelson Brown and Carole Sealy who dug into their collections and found some rare and priceless pieces to include in the photographs. Their expertise in the fickle field of pricing their material was also most valuable and should prove helpful to other collectors.

My gratitude goes to Wayland Bunnell for his professional input into the pricing dilemma. His significant contributions to the growth and appreciation of sheet music collecting is ongoing and of great value to both beginning and advanced collectors.

Thanks again to my editor Dawn Stoltzfus for her quick understanding of what I am trying to do, and to the people in design and layout for their beautiful organization of text and photos. And, of course, my deepest appreciation to Peter Schiffer and Douglas Congdon-Martin for their continued support.

Grateful recognition is extended to all owners of copyright for use of music cover illustrations used in the historical context of the book, and to historical personages whose photos appear on the covers. For the fine photography which gives the book its visual life and beauty, and for the expert advice and feedback on military matters, my special thanks to Roy Short, photographer and consultant extrordinaire.

CONTENTS

INTRODUCTION

This second book in the collectible sheet music series examines the phenomenal growth and development of the United States as it emerged from the nineteenth century Victorian age as a budding world power on the threshold of great discoveries. The worlds of transportation and communication were revolutionized by new inventions, and worldwide conflicts started the country on its way to global involvement and international prestige and power.

The first two chapters examine the inventions that changed life in America, inventions that altered communication and transportation. Communication devices—the telegraph, telephone, radio, and phonograph—had many popular songs written about them, some humorous, some whimsical, and some sentimental, but always reflective of American sentiment.

Transportation vehicles also inspired Tin Pan Alley output. America was on the move in the early twentieth century. Trains whisked people across the country, aeroplanes took them aloft, and a nationwide love affair with the automobile began. Many popular songs were published, frequently with historical pictures and themes. Chapter Two covers trains, aeroplanes, and motor cars.

The drama and pathos of war as well as the actual history are revealed in song. Chapter Three explores the songs from our country's wars, examining the propaganda effect on the nation's conscience. World War I alone had more than 2,000 songs written about it—some of it coarse, some of it sentimental, but all of it timely and expressive. Historical cover photos of actual people involved, and of uniforms, weapons, battles, and military units tell the story better than words.

Chapter Four takes on the world of contemporary events. News headlines were fodder for popular songwriters, and songs that were written to order about current events were a staple of Tin Pan Alley. Sportsman Teddy Roosevelt hunted on safari in Africa, and as President, launched the "Great White Fleet," and songs were written. Lindbergh flew the Atlantic in his monoplane the *Spirit of St. Louis*, to songs America was singing. Millionaire Henry Thaw murdered architect Stanford White who was involved with Thaw's lovely wife, Evelyn Nesbit, and songs tell of his misery. Shipwrecks—the *Titanic*, the *Lusitania*—are chronicled in song. Kidnapping, Prohibition, the Great Depression, presidential elections, the Ku Klux Klan, and the opening of the Panama Canal were all commemorated in song.

Finally, value guidelines are provided with the usual caveat. The author would be grateful for the pointing out of any errors that have found their insidious way into this manuscript. Thank you, and ...enjoy!

BATTLE OF
GETTYSBURG
MARCH DESCRIPTIVE

COMPOSED BY

E.T. Paull

PUBLISHED BY **E.T. PAULL MUSIC C?** 243 WEST 42nd ST

NEW YORK

LONDON, ENG.
B. FELDMAN
SPRINGFIELD, MASS.
A. H. GOETTING.
BERLIN, GERMANY,
C. M. ROEHR.

NEW YORK
CROWN MUSIC CO.

NEW YORK
ENTERPRISE MUSIC CO.

J. A. ALBERT & SON, SYDNEY, AUSTRALIA.

CHICAGO, ILL.
F. J. A. FORSTER CO.
NEW YORK,
PLAZA MUSIC CO.
TORONTO, CANADA.
W. R. DRAPER.
COPYRIGHT FOR ALL COUNTRIES

PIANO SOLO
PRICE 50¢

Copyright
MCMXVII
By E.T.PAULL

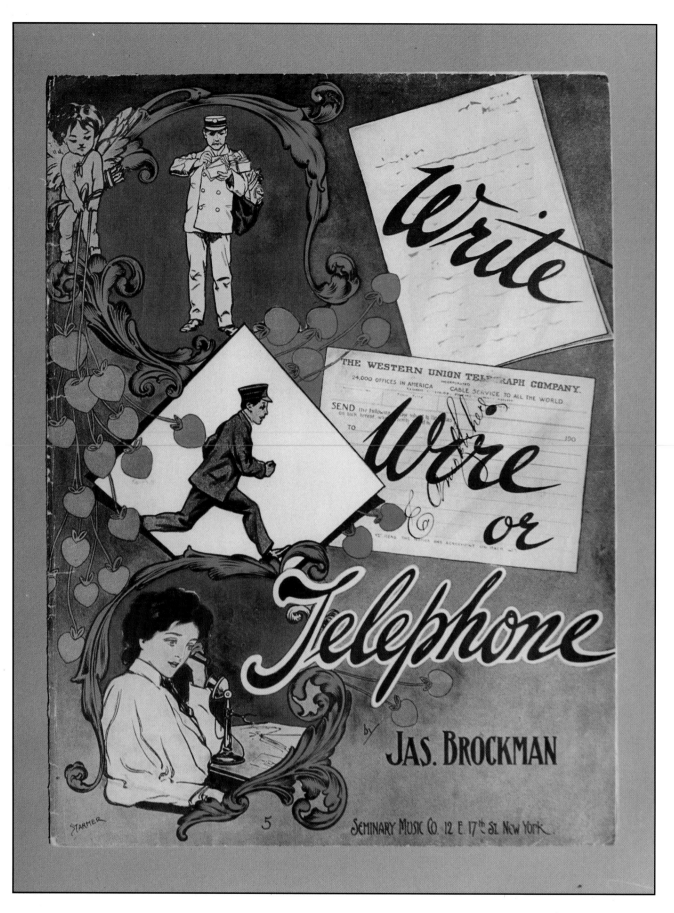

Write, Wire or Telephone
James Brockman's song tells of a lovesick swain who pleads for a
message from his sweetie. (1907)

CHAPTER 1: HELLO, CENTRAL

A continuing theme in popular music production is the relationship between the rhythm of a country's growth and the music that is generated. The emerging technological revolution in the United States at the end of the nineteenth century found a corresponding reflection in songs about communication and transportation devices.

The excitement and wonder of the telegraph, the telephone, the radio, and the phonograph found an outlet in popular song. Tin Pan Alley responded to the public's enthusiasm for these wonderful new inventions, and the diligent sheet music collector can find many songs about them from the mid-nineteenth century onward. This collecting category has a devoted following who collect not only for the songs themselves, but for the historical photos and entertaining graphics on the covers.

In this day and age of sophisticated computer technology, fax machines, and surfing the Internet, yesterday's communication technology seems almost quaint. But it wasn't too long ago that the telegraph, telephone, and radio were the arteries, not only of the country, but of the entire world.

1. The Telegraph

The seemingly ideal answer to the problems of long distance communication was the invention of the telegraph. In 1844, after several years of experimentation, Samuel F. B. Morse successfully demonstrated his wire system before Congress in Washington by tapping out a message to Baltimore, "What hath God wrought!"

By 1860 over 50,000 miles of the Morse telegraph wire connected all parts of the country. A year later several thousand more miles of wire connected New York and San Francisco, when all of the independent lines were organized under the Western Union Telegraph Company. The emergence of Tin Pan Alley and its predilection for timeliness in its popular songs led to a spate of telegraph and cable music around the turn of the century.

I Ain't Seen No Messenger Boy
A ne'er-do-well wandering husband gets no reply to his telegraph. When he catches up with his lady, she shrugs and says, "I would have sent the money, but I ain't seen no messenger boy." Comic cover shows telegraph messenger in plain sight. (1899)

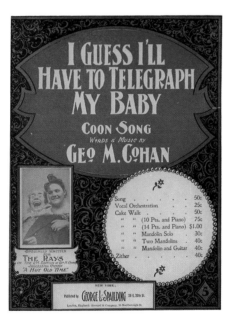

I Guess I'll Have to Telegraph My Baby
One of Tin Pan Alley's first popular songs about the telegraph tells of a stranded minstrel who wires his lady love for money. He waits in vain, and ends up in jail for an unpaid hotel bill. Sung by the Rays in *A Hot Old Time.* (1898)

Old Tennessee and Me
The sweetest girl in Dixie peers from the center of a Western Union telegram to her sweetheart up North in this song by Eddie Cantor, Raymond Egan, and Richard Whiting. (1918)

2. The Telephone

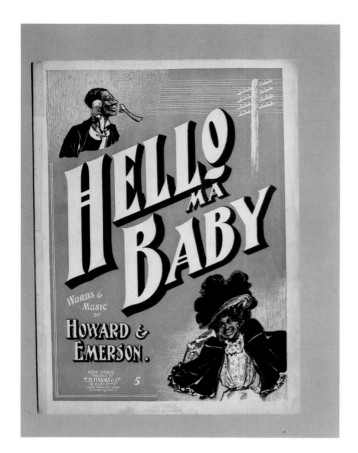

Hello, Ma Baby
The first big hit about the telephone owed much of its popularity to the catchy ragtime rhythm of the tune. Original Harms edition features a black couple talking on a primitive telephone. (1899)

"Mr. Watson, come here; I want you!" These were the first intelligible words to be transmitted on a new invention in the United States in 1876—the telephone. They were spoken by 29-year old Scottish-American inventor Alexander Graham Bell who had patented the first practicable American telephone. By the 1890s the American Telephone and Telegraph Company, which handled Bell's interests, had installed nearly half a million instruments, and the newly invented telephone had become a public necessity.

Tearjerker tunesmith Charles K. Harris had a major hit with his popular telephone song "Hello Central, Give Me Heaven," a plaintive song about a weeping child who tries to call her dead mama on the telephone. "Central" is, of course, the telephone exchange. Another telephone song by Harris tells of children left home alone while their mother is busy at the woman's club all day. The children sing the sad refrain, "Please, Miss Central, Find My Mamma." In a similar vein "Hello Central, Give Me No Man's Land" came out during World War I. A little toddler whose daddy is off to war tries to reach him by telephone at the battlefield.

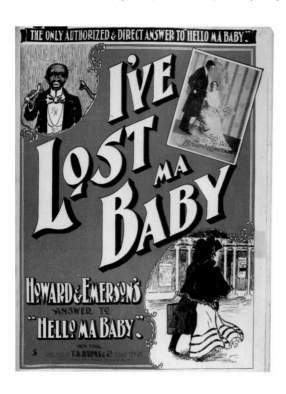

I've Lost Ma Baby
Songwriters Joseph E. Howard and his wife Ida Emerson, in the inset photo, followed the success of "Hello, Ma Baby" with this telephone song about a disappointed suitor. (1899)

Hello Central, Give Me No Man's Land
Al Jolson helped to sell a lot of sheet music with his rendition of this popular World War I song, a throwback to Charles K. Harris' 1901 "Hello, Central, Give Me Heaven." (1918)

"Ring Me Up Heaven, Please, Central" has basically the same message with the childish voice asking for Papa. No telephones appear on this cover, but the photo of singer Myrtle Huntley in exotic garb complete with metal breast cups, bejeweled nipples, yards of pearl ropes, and a headdress of coins is an interesting alternative.

The young lady in the peppy song "All Alone" asks Central to call her boyfriend Georgie at 6-0-3. Yes, three digits was the entire telephone number, and it was given to a real live person, a telephone operator who politely asked, "Number, please?" Area codes and the long strings of numbers that are in use today were unnecessary in telephone's early years, as less than 18 people in every 1,000 owned a telephone in 1900.

Irving Berlin's "All Alone" is a totally different song from the earlier Dillon/Von Tilzer piece. It was a popular waltz of 1924 which also made reference to the telephone in the second stanza, "...all alone by the telephone waiting for a ring, a ting-a-ling."

Please, Miss Central, Find My Mamma
Vintage telephones are used on the cover of this Charles K. Harris tearjerker. (1913)

Ring Me Up Heaven, Please Central
Pathetic tearjerker by Beth Slater Whitson and Leo Friedman tells of a bereft child trying to telephone to heaven. (1908)

Hello, Central, Give Me Heaven
Pretty little Baby Lund is seen on the cover of Charles K. Harris' telephone song. (1901)

All Alone
Marie calls boyfriend Georgie on the phone to come over for some loving as she is alone at home without a chaperon. (1911)

Come On Love, Say Hello
Gracie McLean was a telephone queen, the belle of the Bell Telephone. The boys kept her line busy just to hear her dulcet tones. Cover photo of singer Carrie Starr wearing telephone switchboard operator's rig. (1910)

Someone
Harry B. Smith, Alfred Goodman, and Maurie Rubens wrote this song for the musical show *Naughty Riguette*. Cover drawing shows a pretty little operator in telephone headgear connecting phone jacks into a switchboard. (1925)

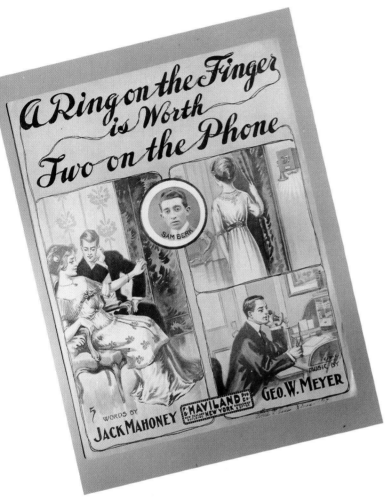

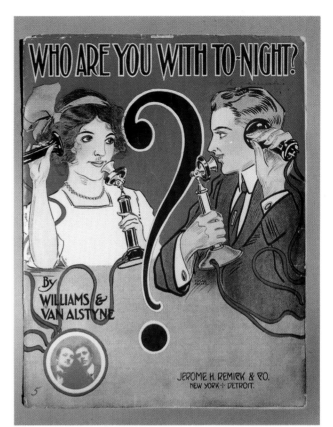

Who Are You With Tonight?
Racy song by Harry Williams and Egbert Van Alstyne tells of a perennially cheating husband who is finally caught by his wife. Small inset photo of composers. (1910)

A Ring on the Finger Is Worth Two on the 'Phone
A practical young lady would rather have a gold wedding ring than a telephone ring. Cover features drawings of two styles of telephone in use in 1911. Inset photo of Sam Berk.

Nora Malone, Call Me By Phone
Lovesick swain Barney implores his Irish sweetheart Nora Malone to please call him now and then. (1909)

Hello Wisconsin (Won't You Find My Yonnie Yonson)
Lyrics in a Scandinavian dialect are used in this song about Hilda Honson calling Yonnie Yonson who "yumps with yoy." Cover photo of singer Emma Cook. (1917)

Call for Mr. Brown
Hotel pageboy can't ever find Mr. Brown who gets lots of calls in this telephone song by Ole Olsen and Isham Jones. (1918)

Hang Out the Front Door Key
Hubby stays out late with his friends after work, and calls his wife to leave a key out for him. She turns the tables one night and calls him at three in the morning to hang out the front door key for her! Inset photo of singer May Vokes. (1908)

Hello Hawaii, How Are You?
Captain Jinks read about the wireless telephone and spent a whole month's pay to phone Honolulu Lou seven thousand miles away. (1915)

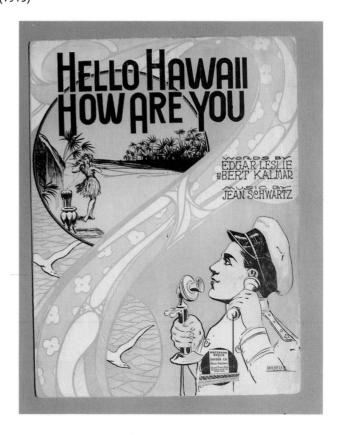

Telephone Styles in the 1920s and 1930s

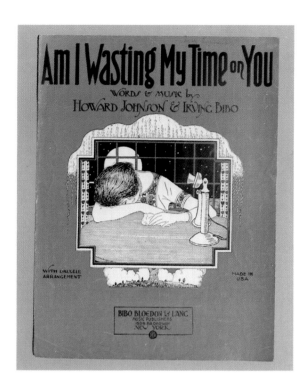

Am I Wasting My Time on You?
Cover of this melancholy song shows weeping lady by telephone that doesn't ring. (1926)

Where's the Girl for Me
Young couple talking on the phone are connected by telephone lines that spell out the title of the musical show *Listen to Me* that showcased the song. (1921)

You've Got to See Mamma Ev'ry Night
Jazzy song by the successful team of Billy Rose and Con Conrad was a popular hit in 1923. Cover art by Wohlman.

In My Little Red Book
Cover drawing shows the newer designed handset with the transmitter and receiver on a common handle. Bandleader and violinist Jan Savitt in photo. (1938)

Hello, Sweetheart Hello
Engaging melody of this telephone song was composed by J. Russel Robinson with lyrics by Noble Sissle. (1932)

3. Wireless Telephony—the Radio

A few years after the invention of the telephone, communication became possible without wires. In 1901 an Italian inventor, Guglielmo Marconi, flying a kite aerial in St. John's, Newfoundland, received the three dots of the letter S transmitted without wires across the Atlantic ocean from Cornwall, England. This breakthrough in communication created a sensation in all parts of the civilized world, and earned for him the Nobel Prize for physics in 1909.

The invention of wireless telephony, or radio, as it came to be called, was the starting point of the vast development of radio communications and broadcasting that took place in the next fifty years. Experiments by Reginald Aubrey Fessenden, an American physicist and inventor, enabled him to broadcast voice. By 1906 he succeeded in transmitting a musical program from Brant Rock to Plymouth, Massachusetts, eleven miles away. In 1907 Charles D. Herrold, another wireless radio experimenter, opened a local radio station in San Jose, California. That same year, Dr. Lee DeForest demonstrated an experimental radio broadcast in New York, playing the "William Tell Overture" from a phonograph record.

By 1920 radio was passing out of the hands of amateurs with their homemade sets into the control of commercial groups. The Westinghouse Company started station KDKA in Pittsburgh in 1920, and A T & T began broadcasting from station WEAF in New York City in 1922, the first station to use paid advertising on the air.

Many more commercial stations popped up across the country, and by mid-1922 one million radios were in use in the United States. In 1926 the National Broadcasting Company created its network web of stations, from which they could send a single program from one point to many other places across the country, eventually reaching coast to coast.

Top Right:
I Wasted Love on You
Southern California radio station KFI published this prize fox trot with an arresting cover drawing by Porter M. Griffith of two radio transmitting towers. (1924)

Center Right:
Velvetone
Old time radios relied on batteries for power until Velvetone came along with their "B" Battery Eliminator that attached to a light socket providing power from the house electrical circuit. This advertising piece was a promotional gift from the Velvetone Radio Corporation. (1926)

Bottom Right:
Since We Put a Radio in the Henhouse
The radio had an influence on all aspects of everyday life including the output of eggs in the henhouse! Cover photo of the Prairie Ramblers, singers over WLS station in Chicago. (1940)

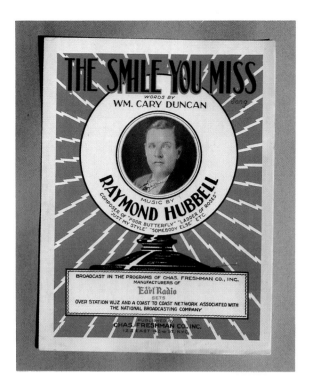

The Smile You Miss
Composer Raymond Hubbell peers from center of large audio-microphone sending out radio waves. This song was a promotional gift from the Charles Freshman Company, manufacturers of Earl Radio Sets. (1929)

I Wish There Was a Wireless to Heaven
An adorable child tries to communicate by radio with her mother in heaven. Inset photo shows Jack Haley (who later played the Tin Man in *The Wizard of Oz*) and his partner Crafts. (1922)

Mr. Radio Man
Little Sammy stands on tiptoe trying to reach his mother whom the angels took away. Song stylist Marcia Freer on cover. (1924)

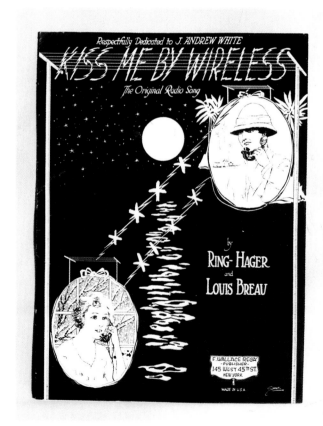

Kiss Me By Wireless
Lovers communicate by wireless across the atmosphere in this radio song. The "X"es on the radio waves are kisses. (1922) *Collection of James Nelson Brown*

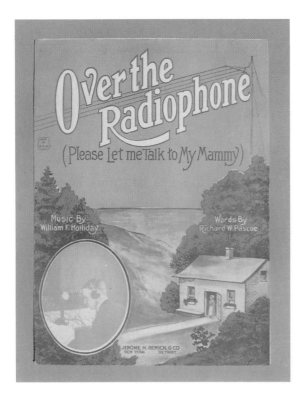

Over the Radiophone
Lonesome man wants to talk to his mammy by radiophone. Inset photo shows man with headset at work on radio. (1922)

Keepin' Out of Mischief Now
"I just stay home by my radio," sings the gal in this catchy song with words by Andy Razaf and music by jazz pianist Thomas "Fats" Waller. (1932)

Loud Speakin' Papa
Comic cover by Wohlman shows an irate wife brandishing a rolling pin at a radio with a speaker-horn. The music has a lowdown blues quality and threatening lyrics sung by Mamma, "…I'm gonna twist your aerial and bust your horn!" Successfully introduced by Ziegfeld stars Van & Schenck. (1925)

Music could be heard any hour of the day on the radio, and a public that formerly bought sheet music for gatherings around the old parlor piano now gathered around the radio to hear popular singers and bands. As sheet music sales dropped, fears were rampant in Tin Pan Alley that radio would prove to be the death knell for sheet music sales.

But by the 1930s radio performers had given new impetus to sales. Hit songs were now being popularized on the radio, rather than by live vaudeville stars on stage as in the old days. Singers and songs often became overnight sensations because of their national exposure on network radio. Demand for sheet music increased sales across the country as people rushed out to buy the latest song they heard on the airwaves. Most of the songs had a shorter life than in pre-radio days, but new ones quickly took their place.

Radio's demand for music was insatiable, and dance bands proliferated on the airwaves. Sheet music with photos of early bands on the cover is a burgeoning area in collectibles. Popular bands featured on radio included the Coon-Sanders Nighthawks, Ina Ray Hutton's All Girl Orchestra, and the orchestras of Vincent Lopez, Abe Lyman, Ted Lewis, Jean Goldkette, Isham Jones, and Horace Heidt. Rudy Vallee's Connecticut Yankees Orchestra, and the Paul Whiteman and Guy Lombardo orchestras appeared on many sheet music covers. They had a large public following who bought their sheet music and records. Lucky Strike's "Your Hit Parade" started in 1935, playing the top tunes of the week, also helping to accelerate sheet music sales.

Gem O' My Heart
Guy Lombardo and his Radio Follies
Orchestra were a regular feature over the
Columbia Broadcasting System in the Radio
Follies Hour. (1930)

There's Something in Your Eyes
Russ Columbo, a handsome bandleader and singer on radio, ended
his promising career when he died prematurely from a gunshot
wound while handling a presumably unloaded duelling pistol in
1934. (1931)

By the Fireside
Rudy Vallee led his band, the Connecticut Yankees, in a weekly radio
show in the late 1920s. As a popular singing idol he used a
megaphone in public appearances to project his soft voice. (1931)

When the Moon Comes Over the Mountain
Kate Smith's familiar signature theme song introduced her popular
radio show in the 1930s. (1931)

"Good evening, Mr. and Mrs. America, and all the ships at sea," was the familiar radio greeting of news reporter and columnist Walter Winchell. His Sunday night radio broadcast reached up to twenty million listeners. Appropriately, a 1939 song was dedicated to Winchell with the title "Mr. and Mrs. America" by Ray Henderson and Paul Webster. Other songs with Winchell's picture on cover were "Mrs. Winchell's Boy," and "Things I Never Knew Till Now," which Winchell wrote with Al Vain and Sid Kuller.

A drawing of the famous New York City landmark Radio City Music Hall appears on the covers of songs from the 1937 movie *Radio City Revels*. This towering seventy story office building and theater in Rockefeller Center opened its doors in 1932 with an exhibition showing the first thirteen years of radio progress. The ultra streamlined Art Deco interior was designed by Donald Deskey with a six-story grand foyer embellished with huge chandeliers of Lalique glass reflected in floor-to-ceiling mirrors, and a grand staircase leading to a sumptuous auditorium with three balconies. It came perilously close to being destroyed by the wrecker's ball, but through the efforts of concerned citizens it was saved and gained landmark status in 1985 as a prime example of the Art Deco style.

Mem'ries
This theme song of the Philco Radio Hour has cover photos of soprano Jessica Dragonette, conductor Harold Sanford, and the show's host, Henry M. Neely, who introduced the music. (1928)

I Wanna Be in Winchell's Column
Veteran newspaperman Walter Winchell appeared in this 20th Century-Fox movie. On cover, left to right, are Winchell, Simone Simon, and Ben Bernie. Bert Lahr and Joan Davis at bottom. (1937)

There's a New Moon
Many famous radio stars made cameo appearances in the RKO Radio Picture *Radio City Revels*. Cover shows Radio City Music Hall looming in background. (1937)

The 1932 motion picture *The Big Broadcast* was the first in a series of four *Big Broadcast* movies that cashed in on the popularity of radio stars. Bing Crosby starred with radio personalities George Burns and Gracie Allen, the Boswell Sisters, the Mills Brothers, and Kate Smith. *The Big Broadcast of 1936* again featured Bing Crosby's singing, and the all-star cast included Jack Oakie, Ethel Merman, Burns and Allen, and Amos 'n' Andy.

Popular radio comedian Jack Benny starred in *The Big Broadcast of 1937* along with Burns and Allen, Martha Raye, Bob Burns, Benny Goodman and his orchestra, Larry Adler playing his harmonica, and maestro Leopold Stokowski. Bob Hope made his film debut in *The Big Broadcast of 1938*, singing what later became his signature song, "Thanks for the Memory." The Leo Robin and Ralph Rainger hit song won an Academy Award that year.

Singer Kenny Baker was lured from a career as a radio singer into the movies. He was a regular vocalist on the Jack Benny show, also singing on the Texaco Star Theater show, and Fred Allen's radio show, before moving on to his own show. He was featured in a string of successful movies in the 1930s and 1940s.

The *Amos 'n' Andy* show was a big hit on radio with its amusing Negro characters impersonated by Freeman Gosden as Amos and Charles Correll as Andy. They started the show on network radio in 1929 performing their dialect comedy five times a week.

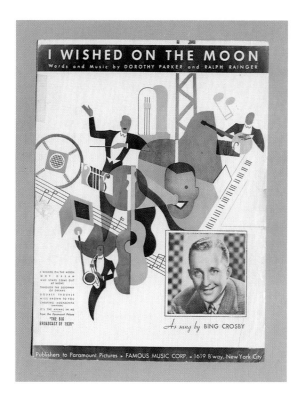

I Wished on the Moon
Song from another Paramount movie that capitalized on the popularity of radio stars, *The Big Broadcast of 1936*, has photo inset of Crosby, and clever artwork done in the abstract Cubism style. (1935)

Please
Bing Crosby popularized this song in Paramount Picture's all-star film *The Big Broadcast*. Cover photo shows many of the radio personalities who appeared in the movie. (1932)

Here's Love in Your Eye
Hit song by Robin and Rainger from *The Big Broadcast of 1937* has cover photo of comedian Jack Benny framed by small photos of other radio performers who contributed to the success of the movie. (1936)

Thanks for the Memory
Shirley Ross's photo is on the cover of this song from Paramount's *Big Broadcast of 1938*. To her left is a clever caricature of young Bob Hope who sang the song in the movie, and drawings of Ben Blue, W. C. Fields, and Martha Raye. (1937)

Check and Double Check
This song title is a phrase made famous by Amos 'n' Andy on the Pepsodent sponsored show over NBC. Gosden and Correll appear in blackface on cover. (1930)

Remember Me
Talented Kenny Baker smiles from the cover of this Academy Award nominated song by Al Dubin and Harry Warren from the Warner Brothers movie *Mr. Dodd Takes the Air*. (1937)

Many other popular radio personalities can be found on music covers including Phil Baker, Eddie Cantor, Bing Crosby, Dennis Day, Ruth Etting, Jane Froman, and Fred Waring. A song presented by any of these major stars reached a huge buying public for both sheet music and recordings.

Serialized dramas called "soap operas" made their debut on radio in the thirties. Their principal sponsors were soap companies, hence the name that is still in use today for televised dramas. The soap operas focused on the difficulties of everyday life with emphasis on romantic liaisons, and the plots took many months to unravel ensuring a faithful following of housewives and booming sales of advertised commodities.

The playing of contemporary popular music on radio was curtailed in the late 1930s when the songwriter members of ASCAP (The American Society of Composers, Authors, and Publishers) demanded royalties for any of their copyrighted songs that were played on radio, and broadcasters wouldn't agree to the fees and instead relied on non-copyright music and public domain folk songs. The golden age of radio which started about 1925 was on the wane, and by 1950 met its demise when television came into prominence as the new medium of entertainment.

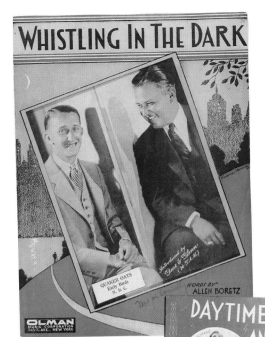

Whistling in the Dark
Gene and Glenn introduced this song on NBC's *Early Birds* show sponsored by Quaker Oats over local station WTAM. (1931)

Lonely Heart
Today's Children was a popular radio soap opera starring Eileen Moran (lower right), sponsored by Pillsbury Flour Mills Company. (1936)

Daytime, Nighttime and You
Al Pearce was the popular emcee of the *Happy Go Lucky Hour* over station KFRC in San Francisco. Cover photo shows Pearce flanked by his gang of performers. (1934)

The Dream in My Heart
Leading players appear on the cover of song from the serial drama *One Man's Family*, the continuing story of Henry Barbour, a San Francisco stockbroker, his wife Frances, and their five children. The popular show started in 1933, and aired for twenty-seven years and 3,256 episodes. (1937)

Rain
"Baby Rose Marie" Mazetta was a popular child star on radio in the 1930s who later was a regular on television's game show *Hollywood Squares*, and also played the comedy writer Sally Rogers on the *Dick Van Dyke Show* in the 1960s. (1934)

Neapolitan Nights
This theme song of *The First Nighter* played while the host Mr. First Nighter strolled down Broadway to "the little theater off Times Square," with the sounds of traffic and bustling crowds in the background. Listeners are seated in fourth row, center, to enjoy a three-act play introduced by the host. The regular cast included cover stars June Meredith and Don Ameche. The show ran from 1930-1953.

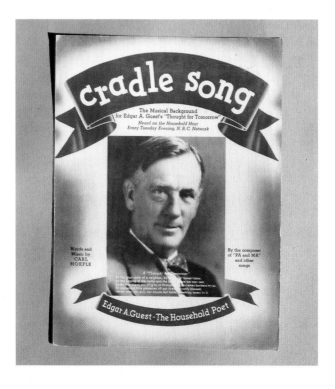

Cradle Song
Poet Edgar Guest offered his words of inspiration, the "Thought for Tomorrow" on the Household Hour every Tuesday evening over NBC network radio. (1934)

4. The Phonograph

The phonograph is a sound-reproducing machine which uses records, either cylinders or disks. The first audible reproduction of recorded sound was accomplished by Thomas Edison in 1877 when he recorded his own voice on a tin foil cylinder reciting "Mary Had a Little Lamb." Generally regarded as a toy, Edison's talking machine nonetheless preserved the voices of many famous people of the time, even an early musical recording that featured famed composer Johannes Brahms playing one of his own works.

Edison's original phonograph recorded sound by embossing a spiral groove into the surface of a rotating cylinder covered by thin tin foil. Inventor Emile Berliner took this a step further in his instrument which he called a gramophone by using lateral grooves on a cylindrical record consisting of a strip of paper coated with a layer of lampblack and stretched around a drum. He later described a flat record which he said offered advantages for copying purposes. This was the birth of the common disk record.

By 1890 commercial recording was established, and had an amazing growth. The forward-looking Joseph W. Stern music publishing company saw the possibilities of the phonograph, and in 1897 opened the Universal Phonograph Company as a recording studio where songs by May Irwin, Lottie Gilson, and other vaudeville stars were recorded.

Besides vaudeville performers, other first-rank artists like renowned tenor Enrico Caruso (1873-1920) recorded on both disks and cylinders. Caruso was popular, not only with opera aficionados, but also with the general public who bought both his sheet music and his records. He began recording for the phonograph in 1902 and subsequently earned enormous royalties. His early death at age 48 saddened the country, and inspired the lovely song "They Needed a Song Bird in Heaven" (1921) by George A. Little and Jack Stanley.

The talking machine went by a number of different names; it was called a gramophone, graphophone, homophone, pathephone, phonograph, and Victrola. As with the telephone and the radio, the phonograph in its various stages of development as illustrated on old sheet music is a prime collectible.

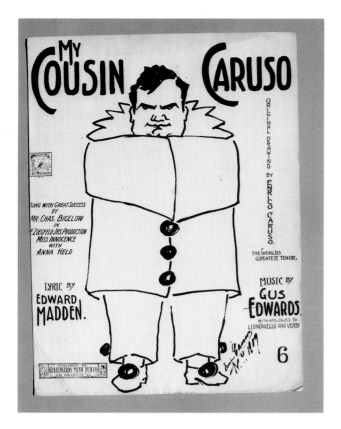

My Cousin Caruso
This song has a cover drawing of Caruso in a "Pagliacci" costume done by Caruso himself for a Ziegfeld show, and includes his facsimile signature. (1909)

Sonora
Exquisite cover by Hayes Lithograph Company of Buffalo, New York, was designed for this advertising piece by the Sonora Phonograph Company. (1920)

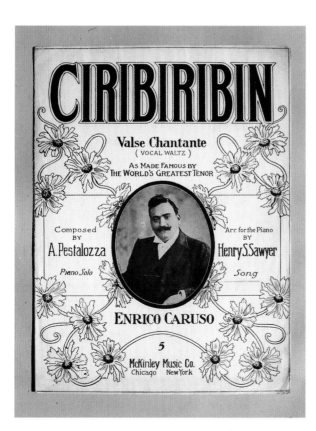

Ciribiribin
The "world's greatest tenor" Enrico Caruso made many recordings of this delightful waltz song published in 1909.

The Sonora Phonograph Company published the song "Sonora" in 1920, notable for the beauty of its colorful cover of a woman and her collie dog in reflected firelight. The back cover advertises the Sonora's tone which was awarded the highest score at the Panama-Pacific Exposition. It is described as the highest class talking machine in the world with prices from $60 to $3000!

The jukebox was a coin-operated phonograph that played records of a customer's choice. It was in use as early as 1889 but was most popular during the Swing music era in the 1940s, and was a common feature in saloons, diners, and drugstores across the country. At its peak, the jukebox numbered in the 700,000s and cost a nickel to play.

Brilliant inventor Thomas Edison affected life in the twentieth century in many ways with his far-reaching inventions. Besides the phonograph he also introduced flexible celluloid film and a movie projector that started the commercial movie business in the United States. Other revolutionary inventions attributed to Edison sprang from his work with electricity that led to the development of the incandescent lamp in 1879 and subsequent development of the first central electric light power station in 1882.

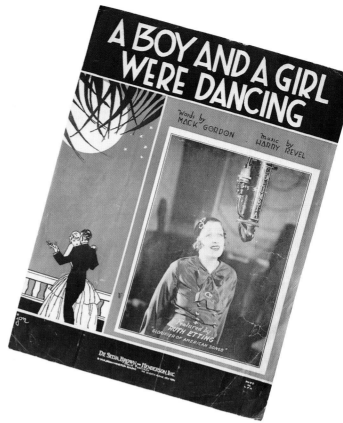

They Start the Victrola (and Go Dancing Around the Floor)
A couple gaily dances to strains of music coming from a wind-up Victrola on the cover of this 1914 song. Inset photo of singer Ethel MacDonough.

A Boy and a Girl Were Dancing
Ruth Etting was an esteemed torch singer and recording star for Columbia Records in the 1920s and '30s. She also sang in the *Ziegfeld Follies*, and appeared in a few movies. (1932)

The Nickel Serenade
The Andrews Sisters sang about the coin machine in the tavern where a soldier and his girl fell in love to the sound of recorded music on a jukebox. (1941)

Every Day of My Life
Frank Sinatra and Harry James made a successful record for Columbia of this song that James helped to write. (1942)

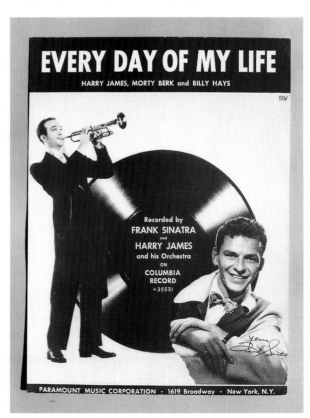

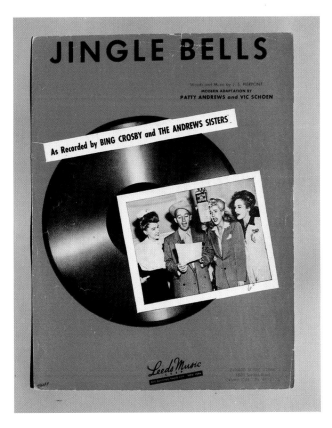

Jingle Bells
Bing Crosby and the Andrews Sisters recorded a lively jazz version of this old Christmas classic. (1943)

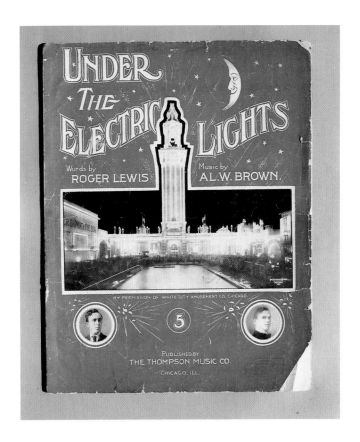

Under the Electric Lights
Cover photo shows the brilliantly lit White City Amusement Company in Chicago. The extravagant use of electric lighting created a sensation. (1908)

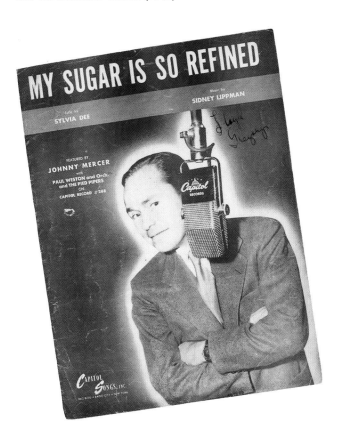

My Sugar Is So Refined
Lyricist, composer, and singer Johnny Mercer was a co-founder of Capitol Records in 1942, and recorded many popular tunes on that label in his distinctive style. (1946)

His Cute Moving Picture Machine
Though Edison was prouder of his phonograph invention, it was his contribution to the development of motion pictures that had a greater impact on the cultural life of the country. (1916)

The Midnight Flyer
The vivid colors of a Hoen lithograph highlight Engine No. 101 as it
leaves the depot in Colorado. This march published by the E. T. Paull
Music Company is dedicated to the Brotherhood of Locomotive
Engineers of America. (1903)

1. Trains and Trolleys

The romance of railroads and trains that whistle in the night has long fascinated songwriters. Wonderful music has been published—great songs with historical cover illustrations—and train buffs, the country over, collect these pieces of Americana.

Early railroads were the transportation arteries of the country, linking coastal cities with the interior, the East with the West, and the North with the South. In 1860 rolling stock totaled 100,000 freight and passenger cars and 1,000 locomotives with total mileage approximately 30,000. After the Civil War the railroads introduced more powerful locomotives for both passenger and freight traffic, and by 1900 total mileage had increased to over 193,000.

The famous locomotive No. 999 established a new world speed record in 1893 when it pulled the Empire State Express at 112 miles per hour, quite a feat compared to the 30 miles per hour of trains in the 1850s. Some of the train songs have dramatic covers of famous trains and locomotives.

Railroad Galop
Photo of Engine No. 277 shows conductor waving at a young lady standing in a field of flowers on the cover of this 19th century rhythmic piano piece. (1896) *Collection of James Nelson Brown*

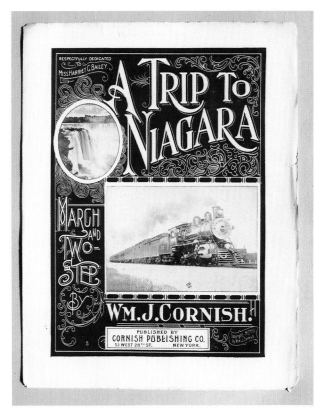

A Trip to Niagara
Shiny new Engine No. 1592 roars down the tracks on the cover of this march. Photo inset shows New York state's scenic Niagara Falls. Dedicated to Miss Harriet C. Bailey. (1904) *Collection of James Nelson Brown*

The Chicago Express
Engine No. 75 of the Chicago Express was honored in this march and two-step written by Percy Wenrich. (1905)

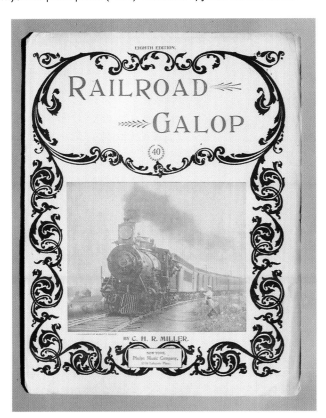

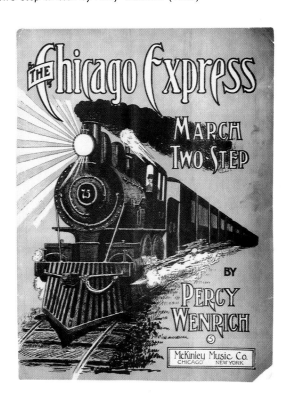

In the Baggage Coach Ahead
Gussie Davis wrote this tearjerker about the funereal journey of a deceased young mother in a casket on the train. Cover shows Engine No. 862 pulling "The Empire State Express of the New York Central... Fastest Train in the World." Inset photo shows Frank Leslie, performer of the song. (1914 reprint of 1898 song)

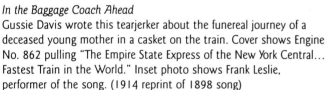

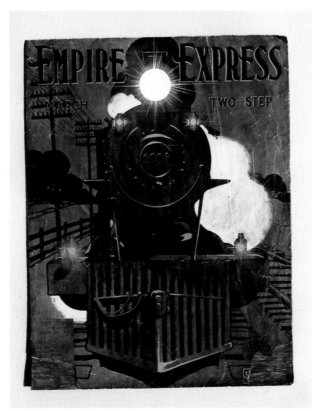

Empire Express
This is one of Harry Lincoln's popular marches written in honor of special locomotives and trains, published by Vandersloot Music Company of Williamsport, Pennsylvania. (1908)

Midnight Special
Superb drawing by W. J. Dittmar ornaments the cover of this Harry Lincoln march and two-step. (1910)

Besides faster service, many of the more prestigious railroads also furnished finer accommodations. Passengers on these trains enjoyed Pullman service, sleeping and dining cars, and parlor lounges. Train travel was fast, comfortable, safe, and the preferred way to travel.

The first modern railroad sleeping car, the Pioneer, was built by George Pullman in 1863. It had a folding upper berth and seat cushions that extended to create a lower berth. In 1867 Pullman organized the Pullman Palace Car Company and began manufacturing his sleeping cars, eventually extending his vision to the dining car.

The Twentieth Century Limited was inaugurated by New York Central in 1902, becoming famous for its Pullman sleeping accommodations which established it as the world class standard for superior rail travel for years to come. Pullman porters were the legendary sleeping-car attendants who garnered the reputation for impeccable service of which the Pullman Company was so proud. They were an exclusive community composed largely of proud black men who handled their jobs with such skill and grace that being a

Pullman porter became the epitome of prestigious employment.

"You Wake Up in the Morning in Chicago" was introduced in vaudeville by Anna Wheaton and the song's composer Harry Carroll. The train in the song travels from New York, through Albany, Syracuse, Buffalo, Niagara Falls, and Cleveland. The passenger enjoys Pullman service, has a nice lower berth, and wakes up in the morning in Chicago feeling rested after a good night's sleep. It sounds like a good way to travel.

Other train songs have actual photos of the locomotives and scenic byways. "Where the Silv'ry Colorado Wends Its Way" shows a locomotive on the Denver-Rio Grande line passing through the eight mile long Royal Gorge through walls of stone 2677 feet high. The words of the flowery ballad and the tranquil scene of the train chugging along beside the river belie the turbulent history of the Royal Gorge.

The Pullman Porters March
Song dedicated to the Pullman porters and to President E. F. Carry of the Pullman Company has fine cover photo of a Pullman coach bearing a company safety slogan. (1923) *Collection of James Nelson Brown*

Pioneer Limited
Another march and two-step in Harry Lincoln's train series has an attractive Dittmar cover published by the Vandersloot Music Company. (1910)

Pullman Porter Man
Impeccable service on sleeper trains was provided by the legendary Pullman porters. This comic song tells of a porter on the Twentieth Century Limited with a wife at each end of the route. (1911)

Mama Can't Pray for Us Now
Kindly Pullman porter tries to comfort motherless children in their sleeping compartment aboard the train. (1914) *Collection of James Nelson Brown*

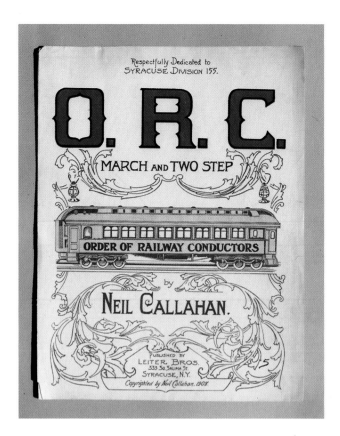

O.R.C. March and Two Step
Order of Railway Conductors is honored in this song dedicated specifically to Syracuse Division 155 in New York. (1908) *Collection of James Nelson Brown*

You Wake Up in the Morning in Chicago
Catchy tune by Harry Carroll, seen at the piano with Anna Wheaton, has a nice blues tinge with occasional use of a flatted seventh tone. (1915)

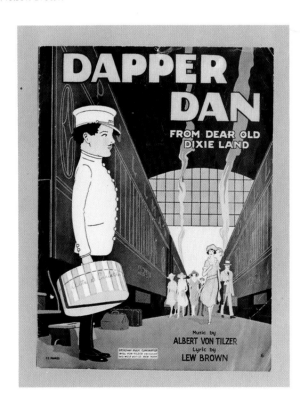

Dapper Dan
Dapper Dan, a fickle Pullman porter from dear old Dixieland, had the reputation of a ladies' man in this song. (1921)

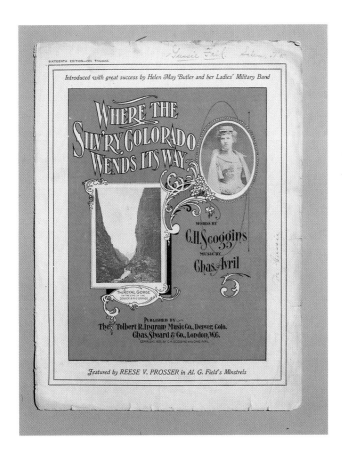

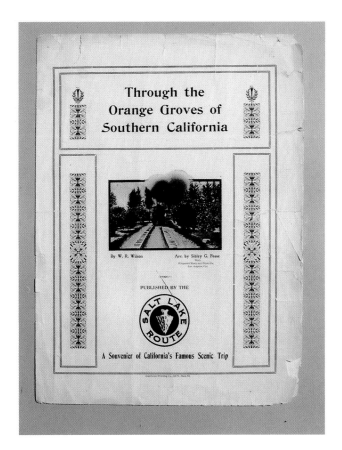

Where the Silv'ry Colorado Wends Its Way
Cover photo shows train chugging through the Royal Gorge, and inset photo of Helen May Butler who introduced the song with her Ladies' Military Band in 1901.

Through the Orange Groves of Southern California
A locomotive huffs and puffs down the tracks through a grove of trees on the cover of this souvenir piece with a Salt Lake Route logo of an arrowhead. (year unknown)

In the Shadow of the Rockies She's Sleeping
Train on the Colorado Springs and Cripple Creek Short Line rounds the mountain St. Peter's Dome. Inset photo of the "sweet voiced tenor" Charles Flynn. (1904)

Rights to passage through the strategically located pass in the southern Colorado mountains was a hotly contested battle between the Denver & Rio Grande and the Santa Fe railroads. Armed men were hired by both sides, rock slides and dynamite charges ruined tracks, train crews were attacked and beaten, and only the intercession of the Supreme Court ended the war in 1880 with the verdict in favor of the Denver & Rio Grande.

"Through the Orange Groves of Southern California," was published by the Salt Lake Route as a joint advertising venture between Salt Lake City and Los Angeles, and has a number of advertisements on the back cover from both cities. Despite its Mormon connections, Salt Lake City was apparently a wide open town at that time with stores advertising liquor, billiard and pool tables, saloon fixtures, and a wholesale druggist with "Cigars a Specialty."

Railway companies were interested in safety, and the Atchison, Topeka, and Santa Fe Railway commissioned a song by J. D. M. Hamilton, the Claims Attorney for the Santa Fe System. The slogan on the cover says "Santa Fe, Safety First," but the actual title of the song is "Rally Round the Safety Habit." No date is given, but it is a large size which dates it pre-1919. The cover features a reproduction of a Navajo Indian blanket.

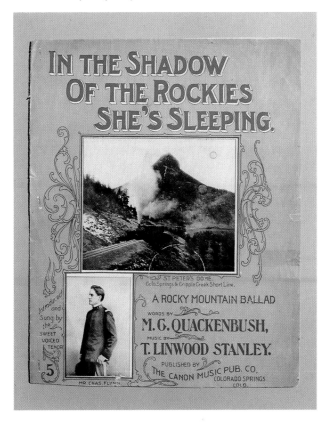

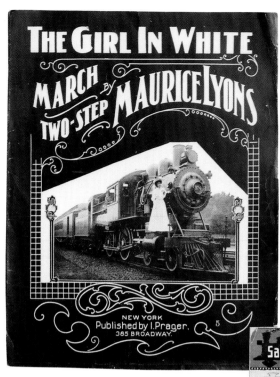

On the Winding
Santa Fe
Attractive cover by
Frederick Manning
incorporates Indian
motifs on a design
surrounding a
photo of a train as
it winds through
the Rocky
Mountains. (1930)

The Girl in White
A beautiful unidentified girl in an
immaculate white dress balances above the
steam piston on the front of Engine No.
974 as the engineer watches carefully from
the window of the cab. (1907)

Santa Fe Safety First
The Atchison, Topeka, and the Santa Fe
Railway published this song promoting
railway safety. (year unknown)

I Thought About You
"I took a trip on a train and I
thought about you" are
Johnny Mercer lyrics for
Jimmy Van Heusen's music.
Streamliner train on the
Burlington Route is pictured
on cover. (1939) Collection of
James Nelson Brown

Hail the Baltimore
& Ohio
The famous
Baltimore and Ohio
Railroad was
honored with this
march written
especially for its
hundredth
anniversary, and
played by an
assembly of bands
at the celebration.
(1927) Collection of
James Nelson
Brown

34

On the Atchison, Topeka and the Santa Fe
Judy Garland sang this lively song about the famous railroad in the Metro-Goldwyn-Mayer movie *The Harvey Girls* which won the Academy Award for best song in 1945.

Riding the Wabash Road
Ultra-streamliner locomotive is pictured on the cover of this railroad song dedicated to Arthur K. Atkinson, President of Wabash Railroad Company. (1951) *Collection of James Nelson Brown*

One of the best known of the railroad songs is "Casey Jones," credited to T. Lawrence Siebert and Eddie Newton. The song actually started out as a folk ballad sung by Wallace Saunders, a friend of Casey's, who worked in the engine house at Canton, Mississippi, frequently tending Casey's locomotives. He reportedly traded the song to Illinois Central engineer John R. Gaffney for a bottle of whiskey, and Gaffney passed it on to vaudeville performers Bert and Frank Leighton. During all this transferring both melody and lyrics were modified and errors crept in, but the basic drama of the story remained and the song became a big hit.

The legendary Casey Jones was a real person. He was born John Luther Jones in Hickman, Kentucky, in 1864, and he learned railroading hanging around the old Mobile and Ohio shops of nearby Cayce (pronounced Casey) from which he took his nickname. He worked his way up from a brakeman to an engineer, and established his reputation as a fast roller. When asked to double back on the run he had just finished, he agreed.

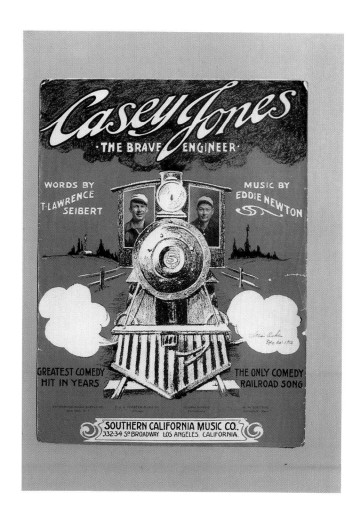

Casey Jones
Famous song tells the dramatic story of heroic Casey Jones, the brave engineer who rode to his death blasting a whistle to warn his crew of an impending crash. (1909)

The date was April 29, 1900. His engine, No. 382, was pulling the Illinois Central "Cannonball" train on this ill-fated run. Locomotive 382 was a fast, powerful ten-wheeler, fresh from the builders (not a six-wheeler as in the song). At 3:52 a.m., doing 75 miles per hour to make up for lost time, Casey rammed the rear of freight train No. 83 whose last four cars were protruding into the main line from a siding. No. 83's caboose was ripped to splinters, as was a boxcar of bulk corn and a car of baled hay. Locomotive 382 then butted into a flatcar loaded with lumber, shuddered and toppled over.

Though Casey's African-American fireman, Sim Webb, managed to jump to safety, Casey was killed in his cab. The ensuing inquiry found that Casey was a genuine hero. He rode to his death blasting the warning whistle to warn crewmen in the caboose and frantically working the reversing lever to lessen the impact. A memorial plaque for

Casey Jones stands in a Cayce, Kentucky, schoolyard, but the real memorial is the timeless song about legendary Casey Jones, the brave engineer.

Other train songs tell of fictional disasters. "Does This Railroad Lead to Heaven?" tells the pathetic story of a small child who boards a train and asks the conductor if the railroad leads to heaven because she wishes to go to "mamma and papa who have gone up yonder." He takes pity, and allows her to ride without a ticket. A terrible wreck ensues and both conductor and child are killed; the railroad did indeed lead to heaven.

Incredibly productive Irving Berlin also composed railroad songs. "When That Midnight Choo-Choo Leaves for Alabam'" had great vitality and interesting ragtime rhythm, and became a major hit. The Pfeiffer cover pictures a moving steam locomotive belching smoke and fire out of its stack, shining its headlight as it rolls down the track.

Casey Jones Went Down on the Robt. E. Lee
Sheet music designed to look like a newspaper covers this comic parody of Casey Jones written by Marvin Lee and Clarence Jones. (1912)

Does This Railroad Lead to Heaven?
Dramatic scene of a large angel bearing a dead child to heaven evokes the horror of the fictional train wreck illustrated on the cover by W. J. Dittmar. (1906)

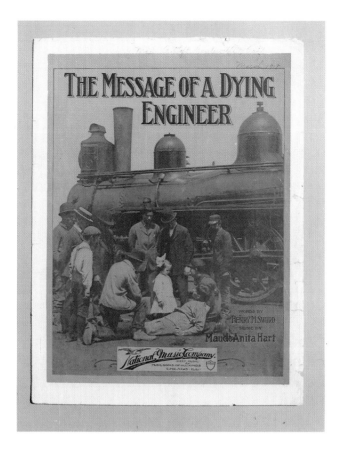

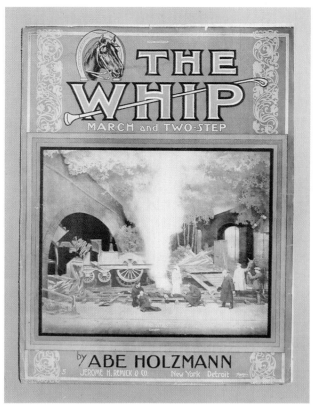

The Message of a Dying Engineer
This ballad tells of a brave engineer who gave his life, springing from the train while the warning whistle rang, to save a golden-haired child who had wandered onto the track. (1908)

The Whip
This march from a 1917 silent movie features an exciting race between a horse and a train. Cover photo shows derailed Engine No. 417 with the engineer hanging from the window, bodies all over the track, and the horse who apparently caused the accident standing quietly observing the dreadful scene.

When That Midnight Choo-Choo Leaves for Alabam'
Irving Berlin's famous railroad song was written in 1912. Cover has inset photo of singer known as Apollo.

There's a Little Box of Pine on the 7:29
This true-life story tells of a mother who passed away while searching for her son, and the irony of fate that finds her son earning his fare home by escorting a body in a pine box, not knowing it is his own mother. (1931) *Collection of James Nelson Brown*

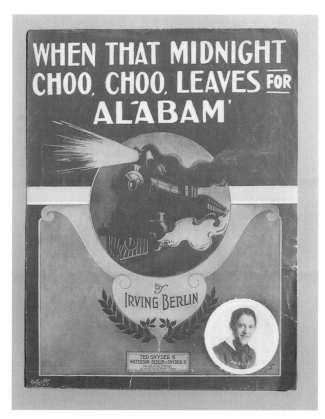

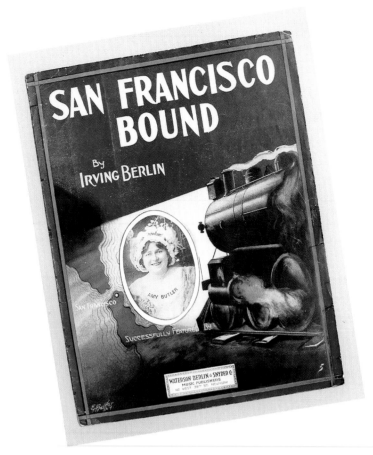

San Francisco Bound
Berlin's accompaniment simulates the sound of a moving train in this song successfully featured by Amy Butler. (1913)

Freedom Train
Irving Berlin wrote this song in honor of the famous *Spirit of 1776* train, a traveling exhibit that carried the precious documents of liberty around the country so boys and girls could understand and respect their country's traditions. (1947)

Public transportation in the cities in the nineteenth century was often handled by streetcars or buses. The earliest ones were horse-drawn, running on the streets without rails. In 1832 street railway service was established by the New York and Harlem Railroad. It was a successful mode of transport, and the use of the horsecar spread throughout both large cities and small towns in the United States.

No less a luminary than Mark Twain wrote the text for the 1876 song "Punch! In the Presence of the Passenjare," with additional words and music provided by A. O. Hand. In the song the conductor is cautioned to punch the fare slip in the presence of the "passenjare," so the railroad owners will get their share.

When You're Down in Louisville
Singer Nora Bayes is pictured on cover of another Irving Berlin rhythmic train song. (1915)

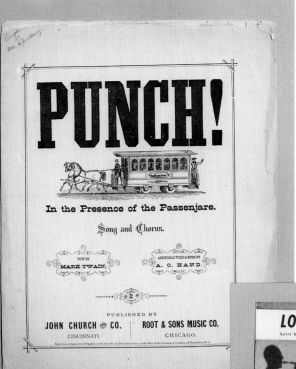

The Trolley Song
Judy Garland sang this rollicking trolley song in the Metro-Goldwyn-Mayer movie *Meet Me in St. Louis*. It describes a turn of the century experience in a trolley car, including a romantic encounter with a handsome stranger. (1944)

Punch! In the Presence of the Passenjare
Mark Twain penned the words to this song with music by A. O. Hand. The trolley bus is apparently on rails being pulled by two white horses. (1876)

On a Good Old Trolley Ride
Songwriters Pat Rooney and Joseph Farrell praise the trolley as a pleasant mode of transportation. (1904)

Love on a Greyhound Bus
In more modern times the Greyhound bus offered the epitome of comfort for intercity travel. Song is from the Metro-Goldwyn-Mayer movie *No Leave No Love* with cover stars Van Johnson, Pat Kirkwood, Xavier Cugat, and Guy Lombardo. (1945)

The Cable Car Song
San Francisco's famous cable car No. 505 that runs along Powell Street is pictured on cover of song that sings its praises. (1947)
Collection of James Nelson Brown

"When speeding along on the trolley I feel like a big millionaire,
A ride on the trolley is jolly whatever you give up is fare.
The trolley's a hummer in summer if you've got a girl at your side
To tease in the breeze, while you're stealing a squeeze,
On a good old five-cent trolley ride."

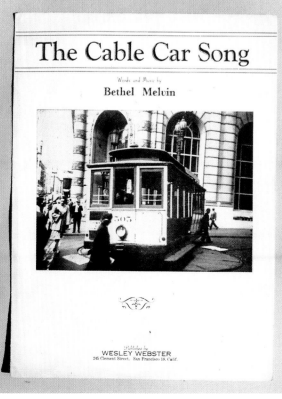

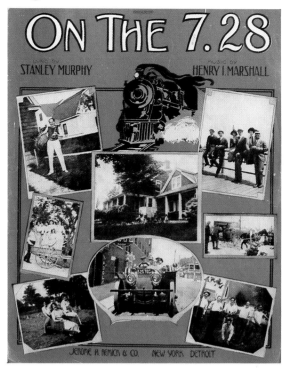

On the 5.15
A hapless hero had a few drinks with the boys and missed his commuter train, arrived home late, and was locked out of the house by an angry wife. Featured in vaudeville by cover star Claudia Tracy. (1914)

On the 7.28
Comic song tells of a happy bachelor who missed the 5.15 and met his future wife on the 7.28. Vintage photographs embellish the cover. (1915)

Let's Wait for the Last Train Home
An eager young man who suggested a late train to his sweetheart during their courtship, turns a deaf ear to his bride's same plea after the wedding. (1914)

I'm Going Back to Chattanooga Tennessee
Man is thrilled to take the train back to sweetheart and friends in Chattanooga. (1913)

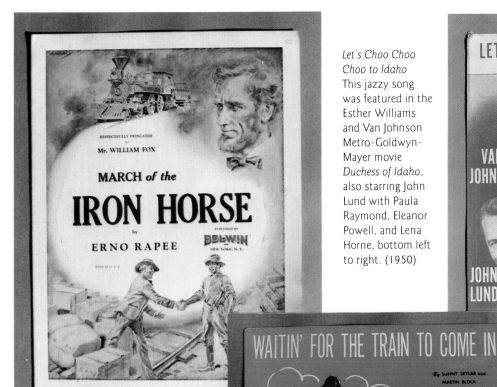

Let's Choo Choo Choo to Idaho
This jazzy song was featured in the Esther Williams and Van Johnson Metro-Goldwyn-Mayer movie *Duchess of Idaho*, also starring John Lund with Paula Raymond, Eleanor Powell, and Lena Horne, bottom left to right. (1950)

March of the Iron Horse
This march was published in connection with director John Ford's monumental silent film epic *The Iron Horse*, a realistic portrayal of the construction of the Union Pacific railroad. (1924)

Waitin' for the Train to Come In
Jo Stafford and Johnnie Johnston sang this train song on the radio show *Chesterfield's Supper Club*. (1945)

Chattanooga Choo Choo
Bandleader Glenn Miller made a huge hit out of this rhythmic song from the 20th Century-Fox movie *Sun Valley Serenade*. Cover stars are John Payne and Sonja Henie, shown with supporting cast—Joan Davis, center, and Milton Berle and Lynn Bari, bottom. (1941)

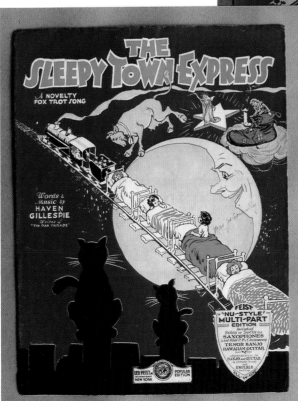

The Sleepy Town Express
Beguiling lullaby with nursery rhyme characters was written by Haven Gillespie in 1930.

2. Aviation

The imagination of man has always been stirred by the thought of flying. To soar like a bird through space and to look down from the great sky to the earth below is a near perfect expression of freedom. The sheet music collector can share vicariously in the thrill of flying by amassing a collection of aviation songs. Many of these songs were written as commemorative dedications to space heroes and are little pieces of history. Others are odes to the freedom of the sky, and laud the possibilities of spooning and courtship in the wide blue yonder. Included in this category are hot air balloons, blimps, dirigibles, aeroplanes, gliders, and fantasy spaceships.

The balloon offered man his first release from being earthbound. Two Frenchmen, the Montgolfier brothers, are credited with the first success in ballooning at Versailles, France, in 1783, while Louis XVI and his court observed. Wishing to test the effect of altitude on living creatures, the brothers sent up a silk balloon filled with hot air that carried a rooster, a sheep, and a duck in a small gondola. After an eight minute flight rising to 1,500 feet, they came down safely (except for the rooster, which suffered a broken wing from a kick by the sheep!). The ballooning craze spread from the royal court at Versailles, and became a highlight of fairs and carnivals. Serious experiments were begun, and the balloon was used to investigate meteorological and physical phenomena.

Jules Verne, French master of science fiction yarns, wrote imaginative and convincing adventure stories about flying machines that piqued the public's curiosity. He wrote about balloon flight in *Five Weeks in a Balloon* in 1863, and about a huge fictional helicopter, the *Albatross*, in his 1886 story *The Clipper of the Clouds*.

By 1900 ballooning had become an international sport, and has remained so to this day. Some of the feats of altitude and distance in the early days were amazing. One of the most noteworthy flights occurred in 1927 when Captain Hawthorne C. Gray of the U.S. Army set an open-gondola balloon altitude record—42,470 feet was recorded on his barograph! He was unfortunately found dead from lack of oxygen on the floor of the gondola when the balloon came down.

The airship or dirigible was the next step in man's desire to conquer the skies. It was inflated with a gas lighter than air, but unlike the balloon, it had propulsion and steering systems. The first hydrogen-filled airship was powered with a steam engine, and was successfully flown in 1852 by a French inventor, Henri Giffard. A number of song sheets commemorate the early airship.

A Hundred Years from Now
Imaginative cover by Starmer depicts his visualization of a fantasy land of space vehicles. Inset photo of vaudevillian Tom Linden. (1914)

Around the World
A delightful film adaptation of Jules Verne's nineteenth century novel *Around the World in 80 Days* starred David Niven as the adventurous Phileas Fogg, and featured this lilting waltz refrain by Victor Young. (1956)

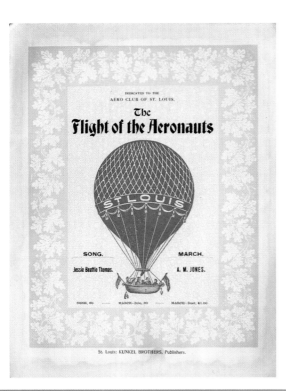

The Flight of the Aeronauts
Several adventurers ride in a balloon on the cover of this march dedicated to the Aero Club of St. Louis. (1907) *Collection of James Nelson Brown*

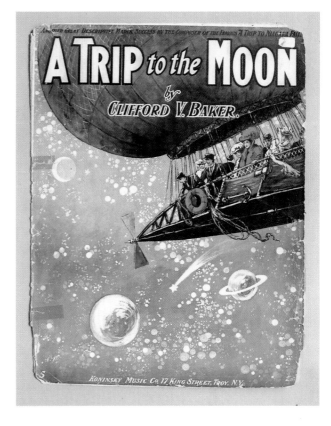

A Trip to the Moon
Outstanding fantasy art cover drawn by Carter enhances a descriptive march composed by Clifford V. Baker. (1907)

Carry Me Off in a Big Balloon
Sue Smith, the Singing Flower Girl, performed this merry balloon song in 1907.

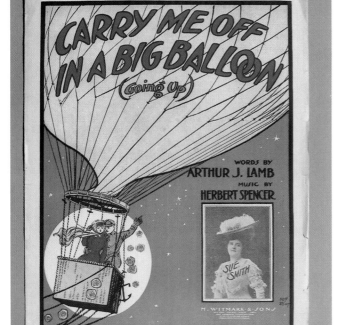

Come Take a Trip in My Airship
Large airship sporting an American flag sails through a starlit sky. Introduced by singer Ethel Robinson. (1904)

"Come, take a trip in my airship,
Come, take a sail 'mong the stars,
Come, have a ride around Venus,
Come, have a spin around Mars.

"No one to watch while we're kissing,
No one to see while we spoon.
Come, take a trip in my airship,
And we'll visit the man in the moon."

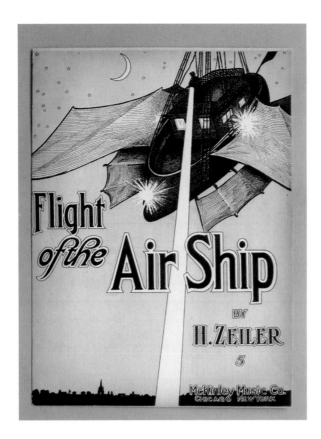

Flight of the Air Ship
A great bat-like airship appears on the striking fantasy art cover of a piano intermezzo by H. Zeiler. (1908)

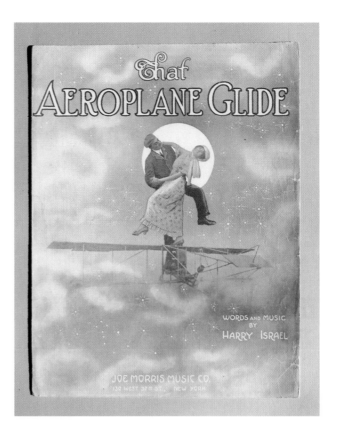

That Aeroplane Glide
Young lovers do a happy dance atop an aeroplane on this whimsical cover lauding the freedom of flying. (1912) *Collection of James Nelson Brown*

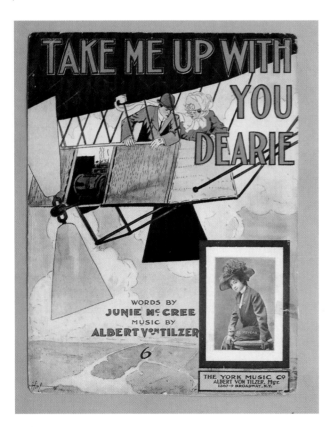

Take Me Up With You Dearie
Junie McCree and Albert Von Tilzer wrote this amusing song about a couple in an airship who plan to be married high in the sky. Singer Louise Meyers on cover. (1909)

During World War I airships were used strategically by Germany, Great Britain, France, and the United States, undergoing great refinements from 1914 to 1918. "Battle in the Sky" is notable for its dramatic battle drawing of biplanes, triplanes, and airships, and a gruesomely graphic representation of flaming bodies falling from the skies.

An interesting dramatic and historical piece commemorates the wreck of the U.S. Navy dirigible ZR-1 *Shenandoah* in 1925. In three verses, "The Wreck of the *Shenandoah*" tells the story of the brave and true men who lost their lives when the *Shenandoah* was torn to pieces by a severe thunderstorm near Marietta, Ohio. She broke into three parts, killing fourteen members of her crew of forty-three. The sheet music cover has actual photographs of the crashed airship.

A leader in airship construction in the 1930s, the Zeppelin Company constructed the commercial airship *Hindenburg* in 1936, with accommodations for more than seventy passengers within its hull. The luxurious craft had a library and lounge with a grand piano, a cocktail lounge, and promenades with large windows. Ten successful round trips between Germany and the United States were completed in its first season. In 1937, while landing at Lakehurst, New Jersey, the *Hindenburg* burst into flames before the horrified eyes of spectators, and was completely destroyed with a loss of thirty-six lives.

Battle in the Sky
Outstanding cover by E. H. Pfeiffer illustrates a midair collision of an aeroplane and a dirigible. (1915)

Hindenburg Theme
Movie theme music by David Shire underscores the events leading up to the explosion in the Universal movie version *The Hindenburg*. (1975)

The Wreck of the Shenandoah
Historic wreck of the Navy dirigible *Shenandoah* is commemorated in song by Maggie Andrews. (1925)

Gliding is another form of flying. A glider is an aircraft similar to an airplane but without an engine. It can both glide and soar—the difference being, in gliding, it loses altitude continually throughout its course, never rising above its starting point; in soaring it is carried aloft by rising air currents and is capable of maneuvers high above the starting point. Gliding is not as effortless as it appears. Considerable judgment and expertise is necessary for a successful flight.

"My Skylark Love" is a lilting barcarolle that evokes the spirit of smooth and soundless flying, "…floating high above with my skylark love." First edition has a cover drawing by Balcom of a couple in a monoplane. A second more common edition has a sky-blue cover illustration by Liesmann of a glider soaring above the sea followed by a trail of seagulls.

Important names in the development of gliding were Otto Lilienthal, Octave Chanute, and Wilbur and Orville Wright. Lilienthal was a German engineer who experimented as early as 1891 in glider plane flights near Berlin. In 1896, Octave Chanute successfully carried out glider flights over the sand dunes of northern Indiana.

Gliders have been used for both meteorological and aeronautical research. They have been flown with as many as 130 men aboard, and were used extensively by the Germans in World War II. The conquest of the Island of Crete in May of 1941 was almost entirely by an air invasion in which gliders played a very prominent part as German troop transports. The western Allies used both gliders and transport planes in the invasion of Northern France on D-Day in June of 1944.

The Wright brothers, who had been experimenting with glider planes, installed a light motor in their equipment in 1903, and changed the history of aviation. On December 17 they launched the first successful flight ever made in a self-propelled heavier-than-air craft from the Kill Devil sand hills, near Kitty Hawk, North Carolina.

The Wright brothers "pusher-type" aeroplane with a rear propeller is illustrated on many sheet music covers. The songs usually highlight the romantic angle of couples spooning high above the earth.

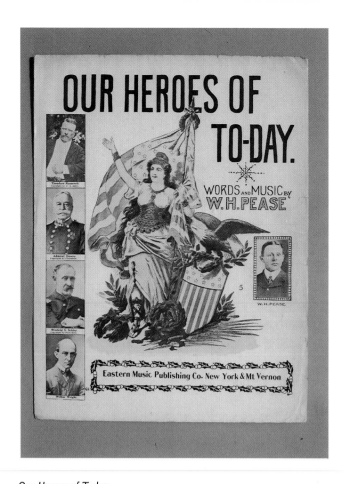

Our Heroes of Today
Rare 1909 sheet music has a cover photo of inventor Wilbur Wright along with other famous men of the day including Teddy Roosevelt and Admiral Dewey.

My Skylark Love #1 (monoplane)
First edition published by the songwriters Bowles and Denni in Kansas City, Missouri, shows a propeller-driven monoplane and a smiling couple. Written in the key of B-flat (two flats). (1913)

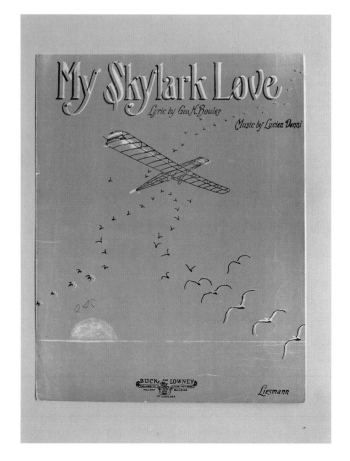

My Skylark Love #2 (glider with birds)
Later edition, published by Buck and Lowney of St. Louis, Missouri, has glider on cover, and is in the key of C (no sharps or flats). (1913)

Wright Brothers "Pusher-Type" Aeroplanes

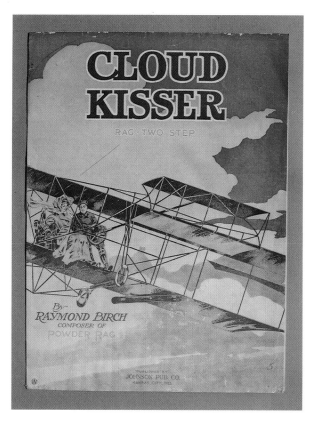

Cloud Kisser
Raymond Birch, better known as ragtime composer Charles Johnson, wrote this instrumental rag two-step in 1911.

Come Josephine in My Flying Machine
Major hit song by Alfred Bryan and Fred Fischer extols the joy and excitement of flying. Inset photo of singer Arthur Aldridge. (1910)

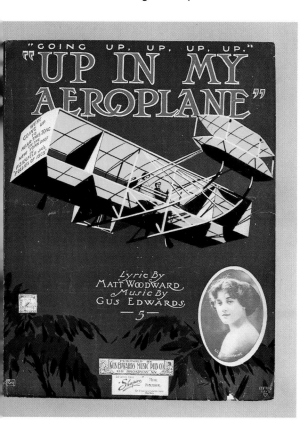

Up in My Aeroplane
Song featured by Lillian Lorraine in the *Ziegfeld Follies of 1909* at the New York Roof Theater has a vivid cover drawing of a Wright brothers aeroplane. (1909)

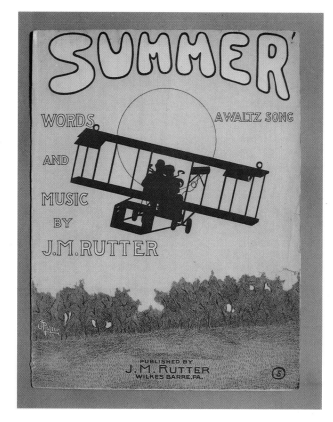

Summer
Artie and Annabel, the couple in this song, fall in love in an aeroplane in the summertime. Piece is composed, illustrated, and published by J. M. Rutter. (1910)

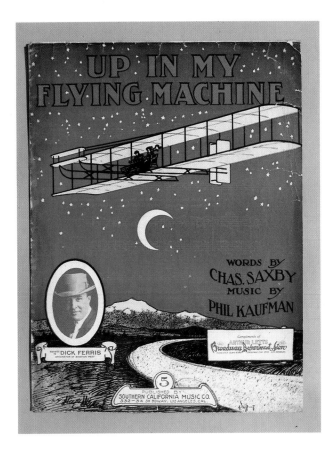

Up in My Flying Machine
The Broadway Department Store in Los Angeles offered this complimentary copy honoring Dick Ferris, aviation enthusiast and originator of the aviation meet. The aircraft looks very much like a Wright brothers plane, except it has no engine, probably an artistic oversight. (1910)

My Aviation Girl
This aviation song was sung by McCarthy and Bates in the show *The Old Town*. Colorful cover was designed by Starmer. (1911)

The Airship Parade
Cover of this instrumental march and two-step by John Fitzpatrick shows a parade of aircraft including a pusher-type biplane followed by a monoplane and a dirigible. (1911)

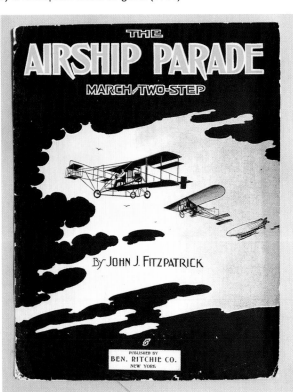

That Aeroplane Rag
Racy ragtime song describes a gal in an aeroplane who tells her beau, "Honey, slow your motor down, don't go so fast." (1911)

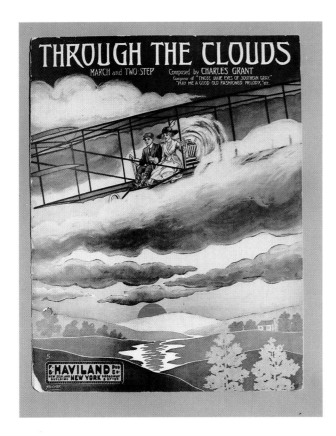

Through the Clouds
Rousing march and two-step by Charles Grant has attractive cover
art by Starmer. (1913)

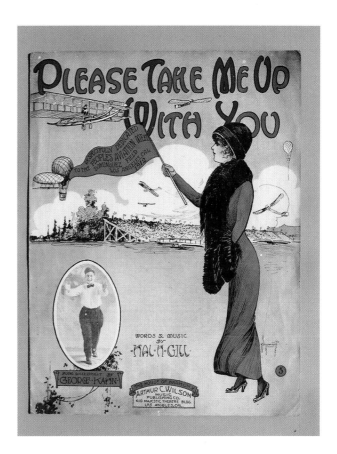

Please Take Me Up with You
The girl in this song isn't afraid of flying, as she pleads for a ride in
an aeroplane. Cover photo of singer George Kahn. (1912)

The Great Waldo Pepper March
Universal movie was about aviation barnstorming in the 1920s.
Henry Mancini's theme song has a drawing of two biplanes and a
photo of actor Robert Redford who portrayed the daredevil hero in
the film. (1975)

Air shows in which flying stunt men showed off their
skill and daring were popular events from aviation's earliest
days. An early air show in Los Angeles is commemorated
in "Please Take Me Up With You" with a cover drawing of a
young woman waving a banner inscribed "Respectfully
dedicated to the People's Aviation Meet, Dominguez Field,
Los Angeles, Cal. 1912."

America's "Ace of Aces" Captain Eddie Rickenbacker
was fascinated at an early age by engine-driven vehicles of
all kinds. As a top racing driver prior to World War I he set
a world speed record of 134 mph at Daytona Beach, Florida.
During the war he became a famous fighter pilot, a daredevil
ace who battled in the skies with Baron Manfred von
Richthofen's Flying Circus, flew the most dangerous
missions, and downed twenty-six enemy aircraft. He earned
nineteen decorations for bravery in action, a promotion
from sergeant to captain, and the adulation of an admiring
American public.

"I'm Glad to Be Back in the U.S.A." was written in
1919 by Captain Rickenbacker and set to music by Carl E.
Summers. In his 1967 autobiography *Rickenbacker* he refers
to the song which sold ten thousand copies in Columbus,
Ohio, and ruefully admits that, years later, he couldn't locate
one single copy.

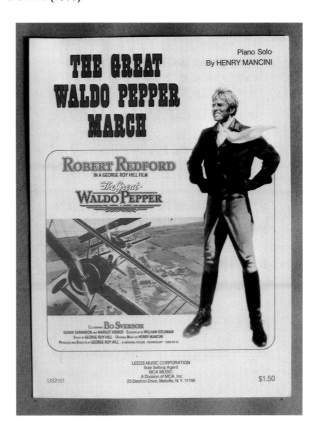

I'm Glad to Be Back in the U.S.A.
Captain Eddie Rickenbacker smiles triumphantly from cover of rare 1919 song with his facsimile signature.

The U.S. Army Air Corps March
Composer Sergeant Harry J. Jenkins dedicated this song to Major-General Mason M. Patrick, Chief of Army Air Corps. Cover photo of what appears to be a Curtiss Jenny flying over a Texas airfield. (1929)
Collection of James Nelson Brown

Glenn Curtiss was another American pioneer in aviation. He flew the first successful seaplane in 1911, and built the first flying boat. His factory manufactured thousands of military seaplanes in World War I, and developed the NC-4 flying boat for the Navy. Curtiss is honored on the sheet music "King of the Air," "The Air King," and "Golden Flyer."

The record for the first transatlantic flight with stopoffs belongs to the U.S. Navy Flying-Boat NC-4 (Navy-Curtiss Number 4). On May 8, 1919, three U.S. Navy NC seaplanes, dubbed "Nancy Boats" by the press, departed Rockaway, New York, to complete the first flight across the Atlantic, stopping at Newfoundland, the Azores, and Portugal. The NC-4, commanded by Lieutenant Commander Albert C. Read arrived in Plymouth, England, 23 days later. Getting there took months of preparation and fifty-two hours of actual flight time through monstrous conditions that contributed to the loss of the NC-1 and NC-3 at sea.

Great progress continued to be made in the development of aircraft, and the original fragile structures of sticks, cloth, and wire that were flown in early air shows evolved through the biplane era of World War I into sturdy, multi-engined, all-metal monoplane transports.

King of the Air
Song was dedicated to Glenn H. Curtiss, famous aviator, shown here with his celebrated prize-winning aircraft *The Hudson Flyer*. (1910)
Collection of James Nelson Brown

NC-4 March
March by F. E. Bigelow was dedicated to Commander A. C. Read, with historic cover photo of the NC-4 aircraft and a facsimile signature by Read. (1919)

The Westover March
Major General Oscar Westover, Chief of the Army Air Corps, died in the crash of an army bombing plane in 1938. Westover Field, the U.S. Army's Northeast Air Base, was named for him. Cover shows B-17 bomber and the Westover Bombers, the base band. (1940) *Collection of James Nelson Brown*

Wings of Victory
A B-17 Flying Fortress and three B-24 Liberators are clearly detailed on cover of song written by sailor Elgen Marion Long and Bernice Long. (1944) *Collection of James Nelson Brown*

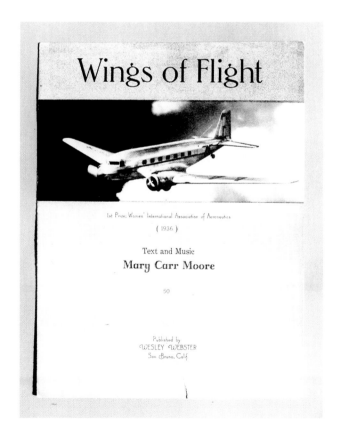

Wings of Flight
Fine photo of a Douglas DC-3 is shown in flight on this cover. (1936) *Collection of James Nelson Brown*

In 1914 The London *Daily Mail* offered a cash prize of £10,000 for the first successful nonstop transatlantic flight, and it was finally claimed in 1919, a month after the NC-4 flight. Two British fliers, John Alcock and Arthur Brown, made a new record by flying from Newfoundland to Ireland, in 16 hours, 27 minutes. They survived a crash-landing in an Irish bog, and were later knighted for their feat.

Twenty-five year old U.S. airmail pilot Captain Charles A. Lindbergh became an international hero when he made a dramatic solo flight across the Atlantic in his Ryan monoplane *Spirit of St. Louis* in May of 1927. He covered 3610 miles in 33 hours, 29 minutes, and 30 seconds. The flight brought him fame and wealth, and accelerated worldwide interest in aviation.

When he and his plane returned to the United States from Paris, Captain Lindbergh was received by President Coolidge in Washington and raised to the rank of colonel. New York City, famous for its wild ticker-tape receptions, tore up close to 2000 tons of confetti as "Lucky Lindy" rode triumphantly in an automobile up Broadway. His popularity is evidenced by the more than one hundred songs written in his honor by both Tin Pan Alley composers and inspired songwriters across the country.

A Sampling of Lindbergh Songs

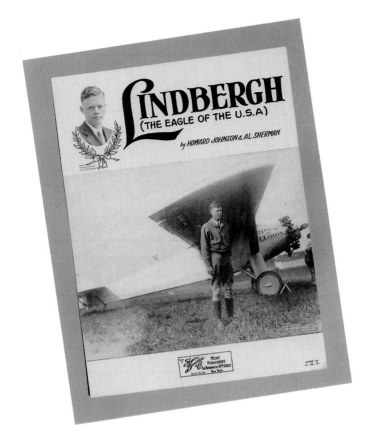

Lindbergh (The Eagle of the U.S.A.)
Lindbergh stands beside the famous plane that made his flight possible, the venerable *Spirit of St. Louis*. (1927)

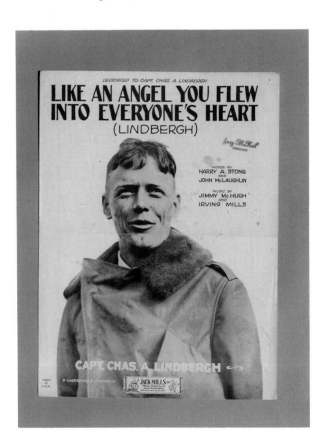

Like an Angel You Flew Into Everyone's Heart
Lindbergh has a lot to be happy about as he grins from the cover of this song written in his honor. (1927)

Lindy Lindy!
Cover drawing traces the route of Lindy's transatlantic flight. (1927)

52

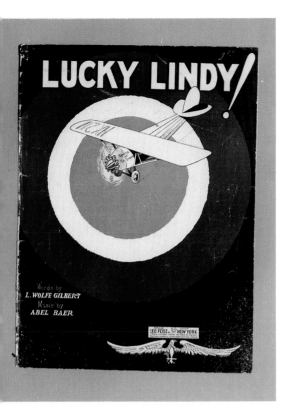

Triumphant Lindbergh and *We*
This double song sheet has two complete marches by Harry J. Lincoln, "Triumphant Lindbergh" and "We." (1928)

Lucky Lindy!
Another popular song written in tribute to Lindbergh who rode the crest of popularity after his extraordinary flight. (1927)

You Flew Over Uncle Sam Takes His Hat Off to You
Songwriters Charlie Harrison and Joe Verges dedicated this song to America's hero, Captain Charles Lindbergh. (1927)

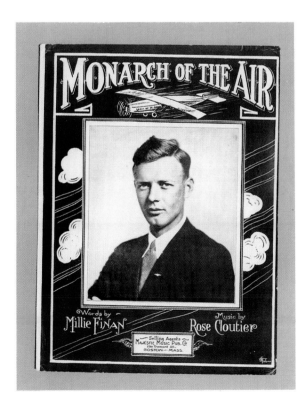

Monarch of the Air
Good-looking Charles Lindbergh was saluted in this song by Millie Finan and Rose Cloutier. (1927)

Explorer and scientist, Rear Admiral Richard E. Byrd, who is credited with making the first airplane flight to the North Pole, also did extensive explorations of the Antarctic in 1929. He reported the finding of new regions, and discovered the South Pole while flying in the trimotor airplane *Floyd Bennett*. Paramount Pictures filmed a special feature about the adventure, *With Byrd at the South Pole*, and the song "Back Home" was played in conjunction with the movie.

Amelia Earhart was another U.S. aviation pioneer who was honored on sheet music. She achieved fame in 1928 as the first woman passenger to cross the Atlantic by air. Four years later she made a solo Atlantic crossing. She continued flying, always reaching higher to establish new records, until her plane vanished in 1937 while she was attempting a round-the-world trip in a twin-engined Lockheed Vega with navigator Frederick J. Noonan. No trace of either the aviators or their plane was ever found in spite of an intensive two-week search by the U.S. Navy.

The exploits of women flyers always attracted attention, and female flight attendants also shared in the glory and homage. In the early days of commercial flight they were referred to as hostesses or stewardesses and were sometimes honored in song. Other aviation songs show pert aviatrixes on the cover.

Amelia Earhart's Last Flight
Amelia Earhart's brave deeds are commemorated in song. The Barbelle cover drawing shows a plane flying over a rough sea with a photo of the aviatrix superimposed. (1939)

The Airplane Flight
Vanity publication by the composer Honorable A. F. Hobbs is dedicated to martyrs and heroes of the air. Shown on cover are Miss Bessie G. Halladay, Major W. C. Lewis, and Mr. Hobbs. (1939)

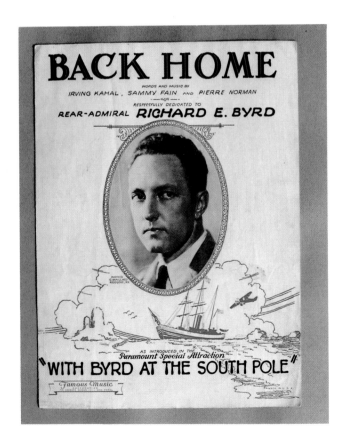

Back Home
Song from the Paramount movie *With Byrd at the North Pole* is dedicated to Rear Admiral Richard E. Byrd. (1930)

Byrd (You're the 'Bird' of Them All)
Song honors Byrd's exploratory flights, "...Over the North and the South Pole you flew, if there were East and West Poles you'd conquer them too..." (1935)
Collection of James Nelson Brown

Wait Till You Get Them Up in the Air, Boys
Lew Brown and Albert Von Tilzer wrote this song about trying to score with a girl who is captive in an airplane. (1919)

Big Boy Jess
The first scheduled Air Express service began in 1927, and Western Air Express was one of the four airlines carrying shipments. Western later merged with Transcontinental to become TWA. (1929)

Hippity Hop
This comic song by Sam Lewis, Joe Young, and Walter Donaldson is about a hard-drinking Irish pilot who "used a bottle for a throttle." (1919)

Come Fly With Me
Three vivacious flight attendants stride across the cover of a song from the Metro-Goldwyn-Mayer movie *Come Fly With Me*. Both Frankie Avalon and Frank Sinatra had hit records. (1958)

Bang the Bell Rang
Ella Logan featured this song in the Universal movie *Flying Hostess*, with the sheet music cover showing a stewardess standing near a commercial DC-3. (1936)

War songs with aviation covers are interesting collectibles, especially the ones with real aircraft. The first film to win an Academy Award was *Wings*, a silent spectacular about World War I flying with extraordinary aerial combat scenes. William Wellman, the film's director, had actually seen active duty as a pilot with the Lafayette Flying Corps, and had the technical expertise to mount authentic aerial sequences.

As World War II loomed on the horizon, Hollywood again took to the air. In 1941 20th Century-Fox studios made *A Yank in the R.A.F.* with some good footage of the evacuation of Dunkirk. The song cover from the movie is notable for its photos of the RAF Fairey "Battles" medium bombers used in the film.

The stirring song of esprit de corps "Bless 'Em All" was the official song of the Royal Canadian Air Force. Several editions can be found including movie editions from the 1951 Warner Brothers movie *Captains of the Clouds* with a cover photo of James Cagney in a leather aviator's helmet and goggles. The inside cover has many extra choruses including an alternative version by George Formby.

If I Had My Way
William Boyd and Marie Prevost starred in a Pathé Production of *The Flying Fool*, an early sound film about World War I flying. (1929)

Another Little Dream Won't Do Us Any Harm
Tyrone Power in helmet and goggles and Betty Grable in a dancing pose costarred in *A Yank in the R.A.F.* featuring this song by Leo Robin and Ralph Rainger. (1941)

Wings
Charles "Buddy" Rogers and Clara Bow, seen on cover, starred in this epic Paramount film that was acclaimed for its authentic flying shots. The U. S. government provided soldiers, pilots, and planes for the movie, plus the use of Texas air-force schools for location shots. (1927)

Song of the Bombardiers
Bombardier, a World War II movie by RKO Radio Pictures, dramatized the exploits of the flying fortress crews trained in raids over Japan. Cover drawing shows B-17 bombers and movie stars, left to right, Randolph Scott, Anne Shirley, and Pat O'Brien. (1943)

You Don't Know What Love Is
Comedians Bud Abbott and Lou Costello starred in Universal Picture's World War II movie *Keep 'Em Flying*. Other cover stars are, Carol Bruce at lower left, Dick Foran, and Martha Raye. (1941)

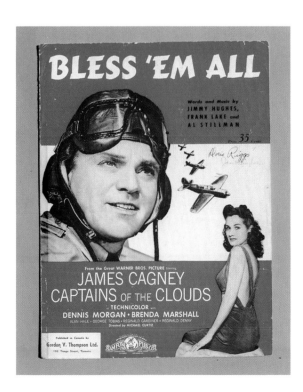

Bless 'Em All
James Cagney and Brenda Marshall costarred in Warner Brothers' *Captain of the Clouds*, a movie about the rigors of life in the Royal Canadian Air Force. (1951)

He Wears a Pair of Silver Wings
This romantic hit song enjoyed great popularity during World War II. Orchestra leader Alvino Rey appears on cover. (1941)

Other good movie collectibles are theme songs from suspenseful disaster movies involving aircraft in extremity. From Warner Brothers came *The High and the Mighty* starring John Wayne as the copilot of an airplane that comes perilously close to catastrophe when it loses an engine on a flight from Hawaii. *Airport 1975* featured a Jumbo 747 jet in a midair collision with a small plane, with no one able to land the big jet except an inexperienced stewardess coached from the control tower.

"Truman Flew to Mexico" is a historical piece written to commemorate President Truman's peace keeping conference with Aleman, and his establishment of our Good Neighbor Policy with Mexico. Four verses relate the purpose of the visit. The cover features a Barbelle drawing of Truman's official plane, a DC-3 named *The Sacred Cow*.

Combat pilots during World War II encountered the problem of their controls freezing up and their planes stressing out when they approached the speed of sound while making power dives. This problem of penetrating the sound barrier was attacked by the U.S. Air Force in a series of tests in the late 1940s.

Charles E. Yeager, a World War II fighter pilot, made the first supersonic flight on October 14, 1947, in the Bell X-1 over Muroc Dry Lake in California. His aircraft was dropped from a B-29, after which he fired rockets to reach 37,000 feet, and accelerated through Mach 1 (the speed of sound). Yeager's comment, "Boy, it sure went!"

Other pioneer pilots of the jet age are shown along with Yeager on the back cover of "Song of the Air Force." Majors Pete Everest and Jack L. Ridley were courageous supersonic test pilots for the Air Force. General Hoyt S. Vandenberg was Air Force Chief of Staff and a veteran pilot of more than 5,000 hours in the air. Brigadier General Albert Boyd, the former holder of the world's speed record, was Commanding General of Edwards Air Force Base at Muroc, California. Boyd prided himself on personally flying all the experimental aircraft being tested at the base.

Pancho Barnes was the colorful figure who ran the Fly Inn just outside the base. Her maiden name was Florence Leontine Lowe, and she came to Muroc as an ex-society matron and pastor's wife from Pasadena, but also had a background as a gunrunner during the Mexican revolution from whence came her nickname of Pancho. As a flyer in the 1930s she broke Amelia Earhart's air-speed record for women, and barnstormed in a flying circus. Pancho was known as a salty character whose dialogue was peppered with profanity, a jaunty hard-boiled babe who wore tight sweaters and jodhpurs and had a heart of gold. Her dude ranch establishment had a bar and restaurant that became a hangout for the test pilots. She was also described as a friendly character who loved and respected the flyers, and wrote a stirring song in their honor.

The High and the Mighty
Composer Dimitri Tiomkin wrote the memorable musical theme associated with this suspenseful movie. Cover shows some of the many stars in the film including the brave copilot portrayed by John Wayne. (1954)

Airport 1975
Haunting theme by John Cacavas sets the mood in this Universal movie about an imperiled Jumbo 747 jet. Photos of the all-star cast stretch across the bottom of the cover. (1974)

Truman Flew to Mexico
Country western singer Red River Dave performed this historic song in 1947.

Song of the Air Force (back cover)
Famous pilots of the United States Air Force are shown, left to right, Captain Chuck Yeager, Major Pete Everest, General Hoyt S. Vandenberg, Major Jack L. Ridley, and Brigadier General Albert Boyd. (1950)

Songs from Outer Space

A Signal from Mars
March and two-step by Raymond Taylor was arranged by E. T. Paull. The beautiful chromolithograph cover shows two Martians on the red planet beaming a light and a telescope towards the distant Earth. (1901)

Song of the Air Force
Pancho Barnes, legendary female proprietor of a social club near Edwards Air Force Base that was frequented by test pilots, composed this song. Cover drawing of the Bell X-1, and autograph by Pancho. (1950) *Collection of James Nelson Brown*

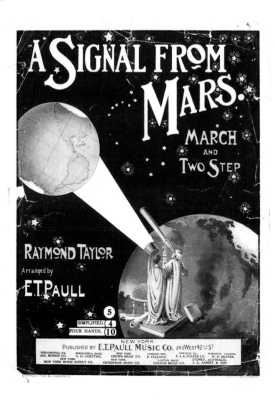

59

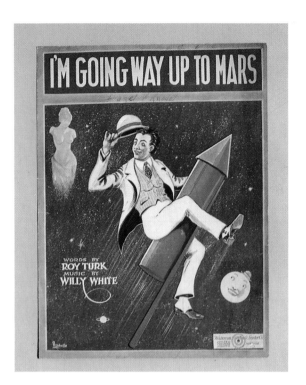

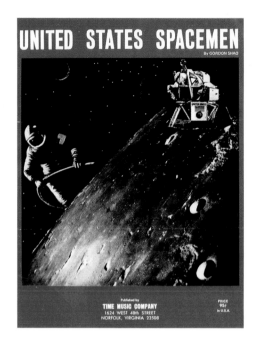

I'm Going Way Up to Mars
Albert Barbelle's whimsical illustration shows a cheerful character riding a skyrocket who tips his hat to a winking, half-clad Venus while the full moon smiles approval. (1920)

Heightened tensions with the Soviet Union in 1950 provoked an anti-Communist song by Johnny Paris, "Bingity, Bangity, Boom! Boom, Boom! (Shoot the Communists Up to the Moon!)." The cartoon-like front cover depicts a rocket spaceship leaving the earth and approaching a scowling moon. The back cover, in a more political vein, offers a choice between two credos—the pledge of allegiance to the United States, or a pledge of allegiance to "Joe Stalin and his political hoodlums."

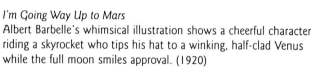

The Comet
Another extraterrestrial phenomenon was celebrated with this march. Sightings of Halley's comet occur every seventy-six years as calculated by its discoverer English astronomer Edmund Halley. It appeared in 1910 and most recently in 1986, right on schedule. (1910)

Bingity, Bangity, Boom! Boom, Boom!
Cold War song was written in 1950 by Johnny Paris.

3. Motor Cars

At the start of the twentieth century, the country began its love affair with the automobile, and again Tin Pan Alley song smiths responded with songs about early motor cars. Automobile related songs is a popular category with collectors.

No single person is credited with the invention of the motor car, as many men were working on the same problems in different countries. Among the names associated with its development in the United States were Elmer Apperson, Louis S. Clarke, the Duryea brothers, Henry Ford, Herbert H. Franklin, Elwood G. Haynes, Charles B. King, John D. Maxwell, R. E. Olds, Andrew L. Riker, Francis Edgar Stanley, Walter White, and Alexander Winton. Many of these are familiar names for which automobiles were named.

The first Stanley Steamer was built in 1897 in the United States. It was a steam-powered, chain-driven buggy with a maximum speed of 25 miles per hour. Both Random Olds and Henry Ford considered steam power but opted instead for the gasoline engine. The Stanley Steamer was phased out in the 1920s because it was expensive to build and maintain, and had the risk of boiler explosions.

The Stanley Steamer
Peppy song from Metro-Goldwyn-Mayer movie *Summer Holiday* starring Mickey Rooney and Gloria DeHaven idealized the Stanley Steamer. (1947)

The Girl on the Automobile
Girls weren't timid about driving the new automobile as indicated in this supplement to the *Chicago Sunday American*. It was sung by Kathryn Roome of the *Piff Paff Pouf* Company. (1905)

In 1893 Charles E. and J. Frank Duryea built and operated the first gasoline-driven motor vehicle on the streets of Springfield, Massachusetts. Three years later Henry Ford completed his first horseless carriage, a two-cylinder, four-horsepower affair. He was involved in building racers for a few years. His most famous one, built in 1902, was the "999" which race driver Barney Oldfield drove at 60 miles per hour, a remarkable speed at that time.

With the favorable publicity generated by the sensational Oldfield exploits, Ford was able to obtain financial backing to form the Ford Motor company and to begin producing automobiles bearing his name. By 1906 Ford's dream of designing an inexpensive car which required minimum upkeep and expense found fruition in his Model T design, which ultimately became world famous as the "Ford car." The popular Model T Ford sold for $950 in 1909, but by 1922 the economy of mass production on a continuous assembly line made it available to all for under $300.

Skeptics who looked askance at the automobile referred to the early Ford as a tin lizzie, and the nickname was used in several songs. "Since Lizzie Changed Her Name to Baby Lincoln" (1927) by Larry Shay referred to the end of Lizzie, the Model T Ford, and the introduction of the Model A, also called a Baby Lincoln.

The Chauffeur
Exciting action cover of an early racing car with right hand drive is by an unsigned artist. (1906) *Collection of James Nelson Brown*

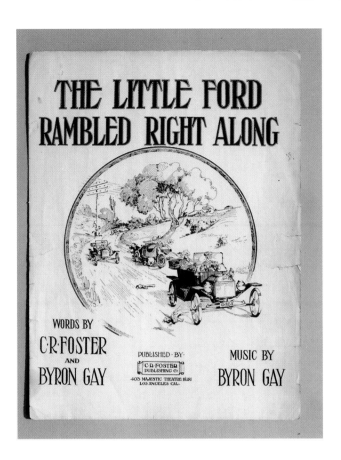

The Little Ford Rambled Right Along
Amusing song tells of a perky little Ford that bested a big limousine on the road, and was virtually indestructible through three verses of adversity. Wagner's drawing illustrates the Ford in fine detail. (1914)

On the Old Back Seat of the Henry Ford
Comic song has a bold cover drawing of a romantic couple "smooching" in the back seat of the Ford, silhouetted against a large grinning full moon. (1916)

The Speed Kings
W. J. Dittmar drawing of racing car No. 2 drives across the cover in a burst of speed. Song is dedicated to the Motorists of America. (1912) *Collection of James Nelson Brown*

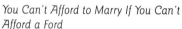

You Can't Afford to Marry If You Can't Afford a Ford
Mary told her sweetheart in this song that she wouldn't marry him until he had a Ford automobile. Composer Jack Frost wrote another song in 1915 with the same cover, "I Didn't Raise My Ford to Be a Jitney." (1915)

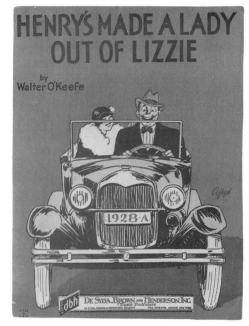

A Ring Where a Ring Used to Be
Edsel Ford was Henry's son, for whom the Edsel automobile was named. The car was a financial failure and only lasted three years. Now considered a classic, it is shown here with singer Billy Joe Royal. (1990)
Collection of James Nelson Brown

The Scandal of Little Lizzie Ford
This humorous double entendre piece tells of Mister Buick and little Lizzie Ford "fooling around" in Jones's new garage. (1921)

Henry's Made a Lady Out of Lizzie
A 1928 Model A is seen on the cover of this comic song by Walter O'Keefe. The Ford has four wheel brakes and a rumble seat.

Happy Days
Show promoters for the TV show *Happy Days* pose merrily around a 1930s vintage Model A Ford roadster on the cover of the theme song from the show. (1974)

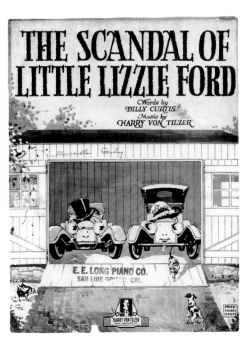

A jitney, for the uninitiated, was a small passenger bus that charged each passenger five cents. 1915 was a big year for jitney songs including "Come Take a Jitney With Me," "Hop a Jitney With Me," "Let's Take a Ride on the Jitney Bus," "Mister Whitney's Little Jitney Bus," and "That St. Louis Jitney Bus."

Much of the early sheet music literature poked fun at the motor car. A 1902 song "Git a Horse" by Reed earned the response in 1906 "Get an Automobile" by Grady Watts. One of the best known comic songs about the problems of the early auto was "He'd Have to Get Under, Get Out and Get Under" with a Pfeiffer cover of a duster-clad woman in an open touring car gazing at her sweetheart who is on his back making endless repairs.

In 1901 Ransom Olds built 1,500 curved-dash Oldsmobiles, and became the first mass-producer of automobiles in the United States. Who hasn't responded to the cheerful strains of "In My Merry Oldsmobile," the famous song written by Gus Edwards and Vincent Bryan? It was written to commemorate one of the first cross-country motor trips completed by two Oldsmobiles in forty-four days. Many different printings are found of this popular song.

Though the Oldsmobile song was the most famous, and the Ford the most written about, many other early motor cars were featured on sheet music covers. An early Buick racing car whizzing past a horse and buggy was featured on the cover of "I Love My Horse and Wagon, But Oh! You Buick Car" (1910), with photo insets of race car drivers, including Louis Chevrolet, the winner of the Cobe Trophy.

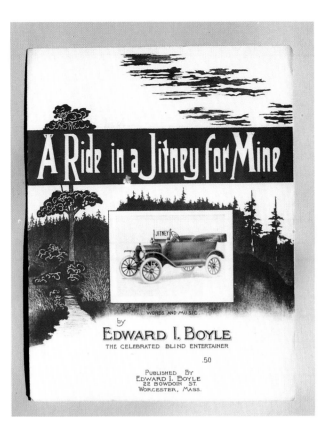

A Ride in a Jitney for Mine
Written by blind entertainer Edward I. Boyle. Miss Layne meets her boyfriend's train but insists "…the trolley is slow, a thing of the past, the jitney has come and it's going to last…" (1915) *Collection of James Nelson Brown*

He'd Have to Get Under, Get Out and Get Under
This major hit song tells of the mishaps that befall an automobile. Cover photo of song's performer, Victor Stone. (1913)

Gasoline Gus and His Jitney Bus
This gay song about the jitney bus, written by Byron Gay and Charley Brown, was touted as a "tremendous laughing hit" as performed by vaudevillians Mullen and Coogan. (1915)

Keep Away from the Fellow Who Owns an Automobile
Irving Berlin warns the girls that in a motor car "...there's no chance
to talk, squawk or balk/You must kiss him or get out and walk."
Photo inset shows Tilford and his wooden dummy. (1912)

In My Merry Oldsmobile #1
First edition pictures a couple in a two-seater open air Oldsmobile—
a so-called "horseless carriage" with no windshield. The steering
tiller has an air-horn attached to it. The vehicle has a curved dash, a
carbide head lamp, and the front-end mechanism and wheel axle are
drawn in considerable detail. Photo of Sue Smith. (1905)

In My Merry Oldsmobile #2
A later edition shows a couple in a streamlined Oldsmobile model, a
large touring sedan with the top down. The artwork is signed by R.
D. Strong '18. (1918)

It's a Rambling Flivver
A flivver is a slang expression for a decrepit automobile. This one
only cost a dollar, and the owner seems to get a lot for his money!
(1917) *Collection of James Nelson Brown*

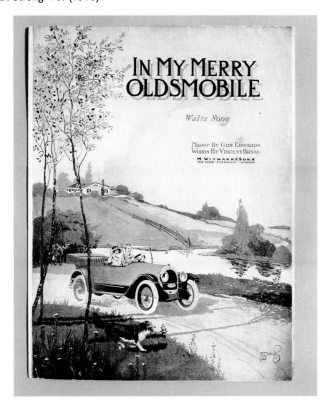

65

Name-Brand Automobile Songs

The Peerless March
Composer Joe Howard wrote this march song extolling the superiority of the Peerless Auto. Published by the Peerless Motor Car Company with an overstamp of Interstate Auto & Supply Company of Davenport, Iowa, a Peerless sales agency. (1917) *Collection of James Nelson Brown*

In My Mercer Racing Car
Cover art by R. Heetfield of an authentic Mercer car is nicely detailed. Sheet music was given out compliments of a Pacific Coast Mercer Agency, Simple & Mercer. (1913) *Collection of James Nelson Brown*

Take Me on a Buick Honeymoon
The Howard Automobile Company published this Buick advertising piece in 1922. Inset photos of the songwriters Ben Black and Art Hickman.

Mack's Swell Car Was a Maxwell
Ode to Maxwell automobile, "...It excelled in the tests that were held, Mack won the race and the girl." Promotional piece has Maxwell logo on attractive back cover. (1915) *Collection of James Nelson Brown*

Ray and His Little Chevrolet
Since Ray got his little Chevrolet he "gets more girls than Ruth gets homers" are the lyrics in this 1924 song. Inset photo of performer Ray Shelton.

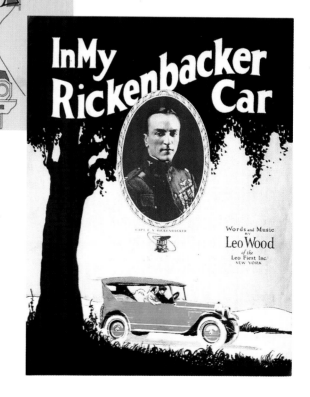

My Studebaker Girl
This song with a great picture of a 1923 Studebaker touring car was a promotional piece with Studebaker advertising on the back cover. (1923) *Collection of James Nelson Brown*

Captain of Industry
Innovative engineer Preston Tucker designed the Tucker 1948 sedan which never reached full production. Collectors that own one of these rare cars report great longevity—they run well after thousands of miles, with good gas mileage, and speeds to 120 mph. Jeff Bridges, on cover, portrayed Tucker in the movie. (1988)

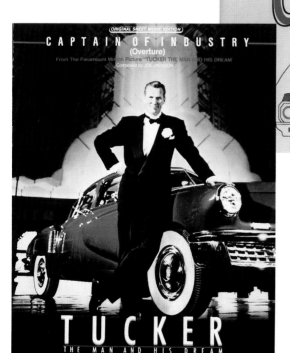

Sing of the U.S.A. with Chevrolet
This songbook has photos of 1964 Chevys on the back cover, and singer Dinah Shore's theme song "See the U.S.A. in Your Chevrolet" on the inside back cover.

Captain of Industry
Innovative engineer Preston Tucker designed the Tucker 1948 sedan which never reached full production. Collectors that own one of these rare cars report great longevity—they run well after thousands of miles, with good gas mileage, and speeds to 120 mph. Jeff Bridges, on cover, portrayed Tucker in the movie. (1988)

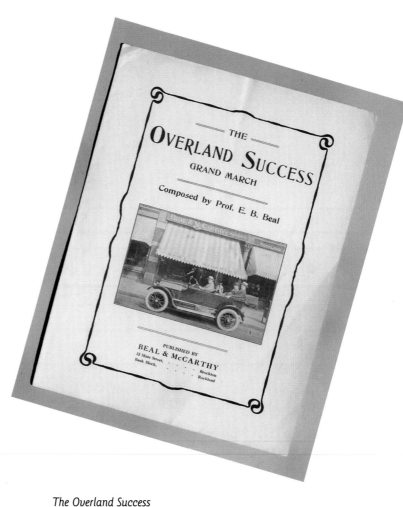

The Yellow Rolls-Royce
Theme song from Metro-Goldwyn-Mayer movie *The Yellow Rolls-Royce* has cover photo of the fabulous automobile, and some of the many stars from the film. (1965)

The Overland Success
Photo shows the Overland automobile parked in front of the piano store that published the music. Piano advertising is printed on back cover. (1914) *Collection of James Nelson Brown*

The Overland Company, manufacturer of a well-built motor car, later became Willys-Overland of the famous World War II Jeep. The jeep was a small open-topped military car first used by the U.S. Army in 1941. It had a 71-hp engine with speeds to 65 miles per hour, four-wheel drive, and high ground clearance enabling it to pass over rough terrain. The nickname sprang from the Army's designation, General Purpose vehicle, or GP.

Through a Long and Sleepless Night
Song from the 20th Century-Fox movie *Come To the Stable* shows Celeste Holm and Loretta Young as two nuns motoring in a jeep with their wimples and veils billowing in the breeze. Supporting players Dorothy Patrick and Hugh Marlowe at lower left. (1949)

Little Bo-Peep Has Lost Her Jeep
Novelty song has a cover drawing of an army private bidding farewell
to his weeping girlfriend because he has to have the jeep back in
camp by eleven. (1942)

A Gallery of Automobile Songs

Motor King (song version)
Second version has words added by Jack
Drislane, and an illustration of several
motorized conveyances—a car, a boat, a
motorcycle, and a plane. (1910)

Motor King (instrumental)
March and two-step by Henry Frantzen has
a Pfeiffer cover drawing of three people in
typical motoring costume driving along in a
finely detailed motor car. (1910)

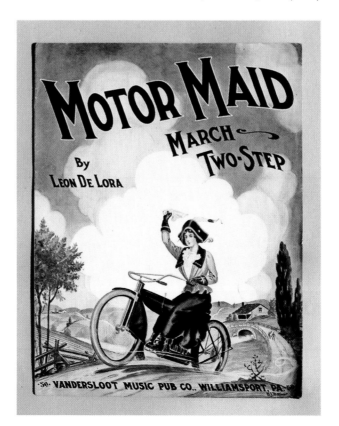

Motor Maid March and Two Step
Modern, indeed! Young lady ahead of her
time takes off on an early motorcycle. W. J.
Dittmar art cover. (1912) *Collection of
James Nelson Brown*

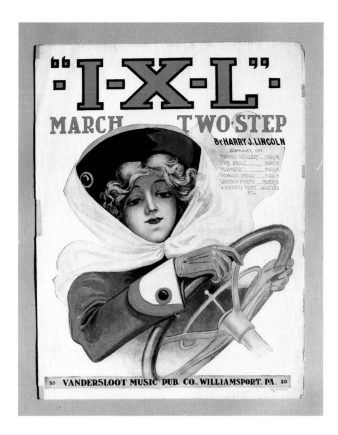

I-X-L March and Two-Step
Cover shows a well-outfitted lady on an outing in an automobile wearing a duster coat, a big hat with copious veiling, and gloves. (1911)

Taxi
Song by Harry Kerr and Mel Kaufman tells of a bellboy seeking a double-seater taxi for a fare who is going out on a date. (1919)

Hot Rod Race
Song tells of a drag race between a Ford and a Mercury that is won by an old Model A that sneaks up on them. Arkey Shibley with guitar is seen on cover. (1950)

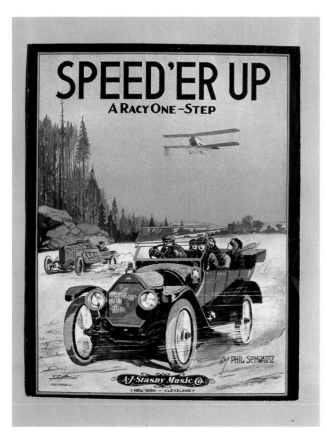

Speed 'Er Up
A racy one-step by Phil Schwartz has outstanding cover art by Albert W. Barbelle. (1915)

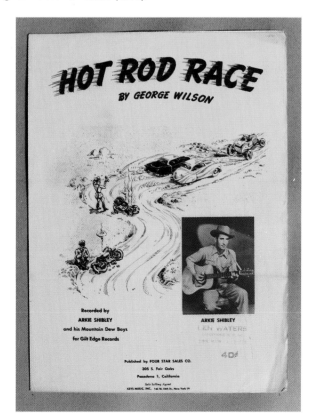

Paul Revere's Ride
Composer E. T. Paull honored Paul Revere with this march annotated
with introductory remarks and section headings describing the
action—"Horse galloping, Cry of alarm, Patriots aroused,
Minutemen assembling, Enemy in full retreat, and Cheers of the
victors." (1905)

CHAPTER 3: THE BUGLE SOUNDS

The crack of rifles and the thunder of cannon were a part of America's growth as a nation, and social attitudes toward war were reflected in the popular songs of the people. Conflicting expressions of pacifist neutrality and militaristic aggression—all the usual "dove" and "hawk" positions that prevail during periods of hostility—spewed forth in song. Songs of protest against tyranny were a part of America's tradition as far back as the Revolutionary War. Battles and victories and heroes, and "the girl left behind" all stimulated an outpouring of song.

Patriotic emotionalism was also present during the Spanish-American War, World War I, and World War II, with reams of music written to express it. It was found that music espousing a cause was a successful method of propagandizing an unpopular political position during World War I. Tin Pan Alley songwriters rallied to the call, and a spate of flag-waving, heart-thumping, tearjerking songs appeared.

By World War II merchandising of a war had become fine-tuned, and President Franklin Roosevelt called upon the entertainment industry to aid in promoting patriotism, selling War Bonds, and romanticizing the conflict. Those were the days when high school lads couldn't wait to be old enough to join the military service and enter the fray.

Collecting war songs is like collecting bits and pieces of history. Fields of battle, uniforms and guns, military and political personages, U. S. Navy ships, and real soldiers and sailors from the conflicts are all there on the covers. The music itself contains the heart and soul of a country at war, the courage, humor, pathos, and fear, but most of all, the fervent love of country.

1. The Revolutionary War

On June 17, 1775, the first major battle of the American Revolution, known as the Battle of Bunker Hill was fought. The dramatic battle inspired Henry B. Ingram to write a memorial song dedicated to the sons and daughters of the American Revolution, "On Bunker Hill Where Warren Fell." American casualties in that battle amounted to 420 killed and wounded, including bold brave General Joseph Warren who was honored in the song.

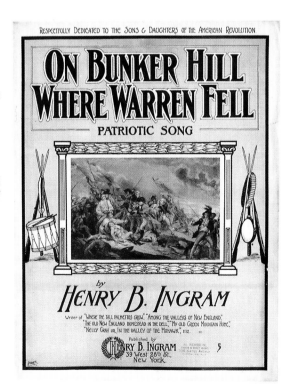

On Bunker Hill Where Warren Fell Song pays homage to the Bunker Hill patriots. Artist Starmer incorporates the scene from John Trumbull's original painting "Battle of Bunker Hill." (1905)

Battle of the Nations
Descriptive E. T. Paull march has dramatic cover of violent battle scene surrounded by flags of the warring nations. Lithography by A. Hoen and Company. (1915)

Paul Revere was the legendary patriot who rode with William Dawes from Charlestown to Lexington, Massachusetts, on the night of April 18, 1775, to warn the Middlesex villages and farms of approaching British troops. His exploit was made famous in Henry Wadsworth Longfellow's epic poem, "Paul Revere's Ride" written in 1863, and again with an exciting march composed by E. T. Paull in 1905 with a brilliant chromolithograph cover of the dramatic ride by A. Hoen and Company of Richmond, Virginia.

Songs from World War I drew parallels with occurrences in the Revolutionary War. The Liberty Bell was first hung in 1753 in the new Pennsylvania State House. Inscribed with the words "Proclaim Liberty throughout all the Land," it was rung in July 1776, to celebrate the adoption of the Declaration of Independence. When a crack developed in 1846 and the bell could no longer be sounded, it was removed to Philadelphia's Liberty Bell pavilion in a place of honor as the symbol of the fight for independence.

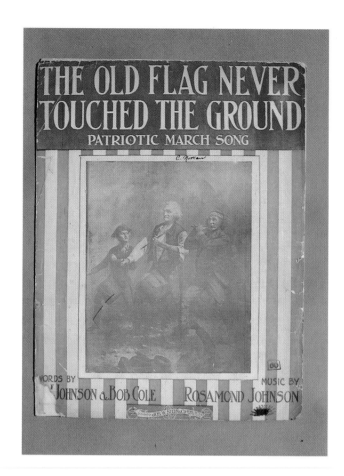

The Old Flag Never Touched the Ground
Patriotic song with "Spirit of '76" artwork was written by J. W. Johnson and Bob Cole to music by Rosamond Johnson. Dedication was to Sergeant Carney of Massachusetts. (1901)

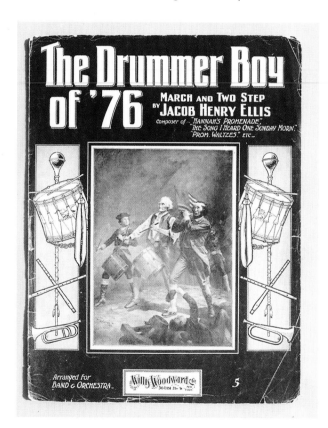

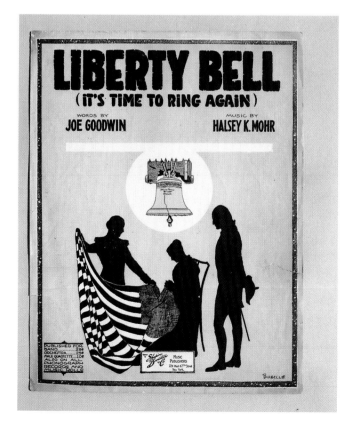

The Drummer Boy of '76
March by Jacob Henry Ellis is based on the Revolutionary War painting by Archibald M. Willard, the famous "Spirit of '76," which shows the drummer boy, the old drummer, and the fifer bravely rallying the troops in battle. (1903)

Liberty Bell
Patriotic World War I song reminds the Liberty Bell to end its slumber and to ring again in the cause of freedom and democracy. (1917)

George Washington's greatly outnumbered Continental army was forced by the British to retreat across the Delaware River into Pennsylvania in 1776. But in a daring move on Christmas night he recrossed the icy river and took the enemy by surprise and occupied the town. Two songs from World War I have cover pictures based on the painting "Washington Crossing the Delaware" by Emanuel Leutze/ Eastman Johnson.

The Marquis de Lafayette was a French nobleman who became an American hero when he defied French authorities and crossed the Atlantic to side with the colonists in the Revolutionary War. As a friend and supporter of George Washington, he fought with him at the Battle of Brandywine in 1777 and at Valley Forge in 1778. "Lafayette, We Hear You Calling" urged support of France as an ally in World War I.

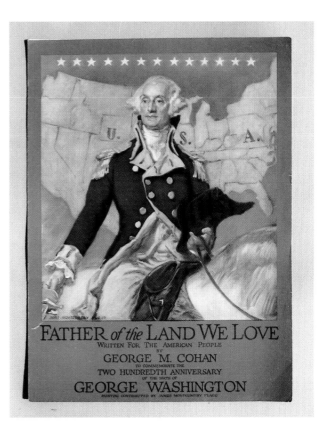

Father of the Land We Love
George Washington, staunch leader of the Continental Army, is represented on cover by famous artist James Montgomery Flagg on the occasion of the 200th anniversary of his birth. (1931)

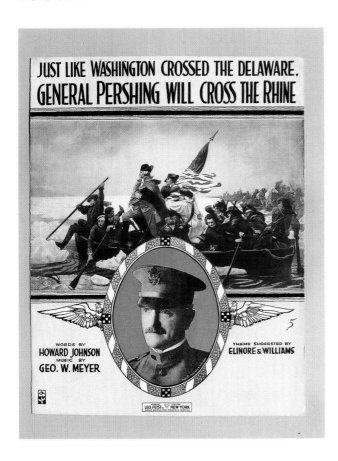

Just Like Washington Crossed the Delaware, General Pershing Will Cross the Rhine
George Washington's gallant deed is called to mind in this rallying song supporting General Pershing during World War I. (1918)

Lafayette (We Hear You Calling)
"...the tears of France are falling, we will help her to smile again, Lafayette's spirit is calling from over the sea..." are eloquent lyrics in song by Mary Earl. (1918)

2. The Civil War

The dissension and bitterness and the sheer heartache of the Civil War inspired thousands of songs, many of which have become enduring classics. This was an era fraught with emotion in which the grieving of America over losses, both North and South, found its expression in song.

Walter Kitteridge wrote "Tenting Tonight on the Old Camp Ground" in 1862. Soldiers on both sides of the fracas identified with the miserable conditions of war, longing for the hostilities to cease, and the song became a popular standard during the war years, and for some time after. Other important contributions to Civil War songs were George Frederick Root's" Just Before the Battle, Mother," Henry Clay Work's "Marching Through Georgia," Patrick Sarsfield Gilmore's "When Johnny Comes Marching Home," Henry Tucker's "Weeping, Sad and Lonely," Daniel Decatur Emmett's "Dixie," and Will Shakespeare Hays' "The Drummer Boy of Shiloh."

The battle of Gettysburg was the most famous battle of the Civil War commencing on July 1st 1863, and lasting three days with tremendous losses on both sides. E. T. Paull's descriptive march is again representational of the battle with headings describing the various events, and has a complete review of the battle on the inside cover.

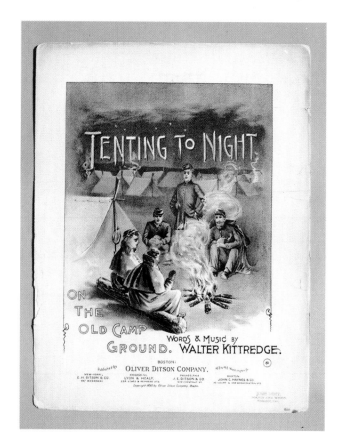

Tenting Tonight
Melancholy Civil War song was written by Walter Kitteridge shortly after he was drafted by the Northern army. (1890 reprint)

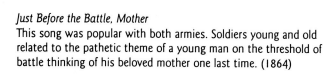

Just Before the Battle, Mother
This song was popular with both armies. Soldiers young and old related to the pathetic theme of a young man on the threshold of battle thinking of his beloved mother one last time. (1864)

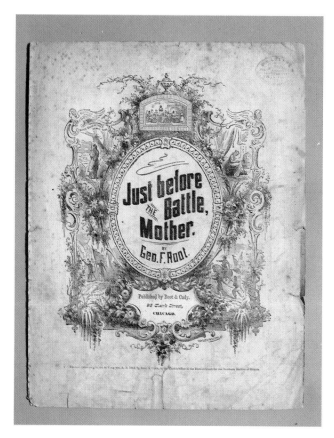

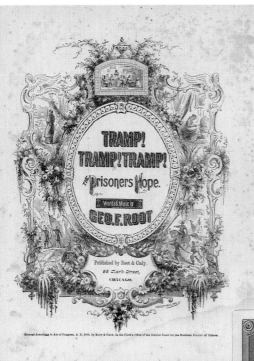

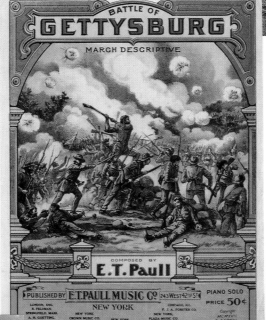

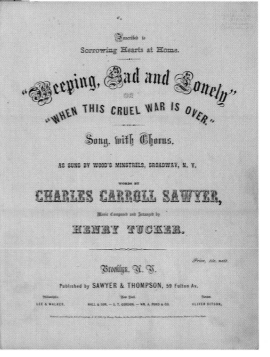

Tramp! Tramp! Tramp!
Subtitled "The Prisoner's Hope," George F. Root's song tells of an imprisoned soldier who waits hopefully for the iron door to open wide. "…We shall breathe the air again of the free land in our own beloved home." (1864)

The Battle of Gettysburg
A. Hoen and Company lithograph depicts Pickett's division of 15,000 troops in their tragic charge up Cemetery Ridge in Gettysburg, Pennsylvania. (1917)

Just at the Break of Day
A soldier captured at Gettysburg is arrested as a spy, and meets his death at the hands of a firing squad at dawn's first light. (1905)

Weeping, Sad and Lonely or When this Cruel War Is Over
Sad lyrics by Charles Carroll Sawyer blend with the music of Henry Tucker in this Civil War song that reflects the worries and fears of those left behind. Gallant optimism is shown in the last verse praising the nation's sons who are fighting for God and liberty. (1863)

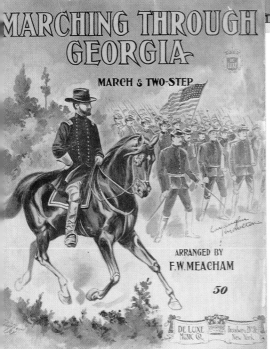

Marching Through Georgia
Composer Henry Clay Work was a Connecticut Yankee, an ardent abolitionist with great sympathy for the slaves. His 1865 song celebrated Sherman's historic march to the sea. (This 1908 reprint was arranged for piano by F. W. Meacham)

After the battle of Gettysburg, a dead soldier was found on the field, clasping in his hand an ambrotype of his three little children. A kind doctor had the picture photographed and published in newspapers across the country in hopes that the family could be located.

At length, the picture was identified by a soldier's wife who had sent her husband such a picture, and with painful certainty came the news that she was a widow and her little ones were orphans. The lithograph on the cover of "The Children of the Battlefield" is an accurate copy of the original picture which was found in the hands of the dead hero, and a likeness of his children, Frank, Frederick, and Alice Humiston.

The song was written by James G. Clark who dedicated it to Dr. J. Francis Bourns, the doctor who led the search for the family. All proceeds of the sales of this music were earmarked for the support and education of the orphan children.

Thomas J. "Stonewall" Jackson was a gallant soldier of the Confederacy, and one of General Robert E. Lee's most trusted officers. He was tough and indomitable in battle, and received his nickname at the first battle of Manassas. He was wounded at the battle of Chancellorsville in 1863, and died shortly afterward.

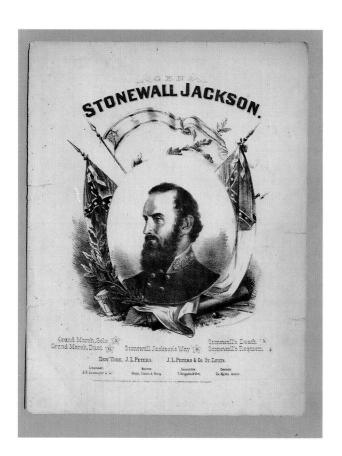

Stonewall Jackson Grand March
Passionate battle song by Charles Young lauds heroic Civil War general Thomas J. "Stonewall" Jackson. Lithograph by Endicott & Company of New York. (1869)

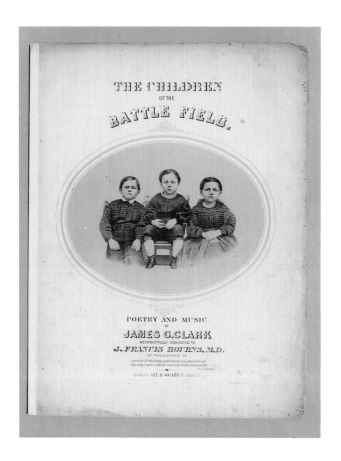

The Children of the Battle Field
Pathetic true life story is related in this Civil War song by James G. Clark with lithograph of the orphaned children on the cover. (1864)

General Ulysses S. Grant was an important leader during the Civil War. After distinguishing himself in the Vicksburg and Chattanooga campaigns, he was appointed chief of all the Union armies by President Lincoln in 1864. He successfully coordinated the campaigns of the Union forces and secured the surrender of the Confederacy by General Robert E. Lee at Appomattox Court House in 1865. He was elected President in 1868 and began an eight year administration at the White House, but after an unsuccessful bid for a third term he retired to write his memoirs. Grant died in 1885 at Mount McGregor, New York.

Touching sentiment and sincerity color a patriotic song written by W. C. Parker in 1895. Three verses speak of the track of ruthless time, "...the lapse of years has hushed the din of cannon's roar and trumpet's blast, no more tread of marching feet ...the foes of yore are foes no more, the gray coats mingle with the blue. One flag floats proudly over all ...the men of gray are now true blue, and boys in blue are turning gray."

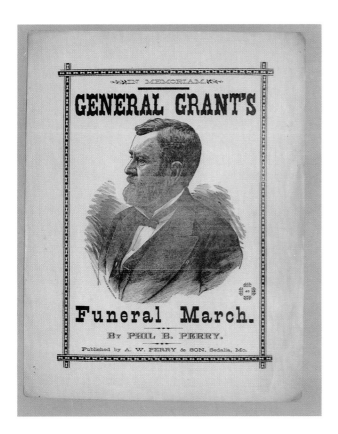

General Grant's Funeral March
Brave leader of the Union armies during the Civil War, General U. S. Grant was honored with this funeral march by Phil B. Perry. (1885)

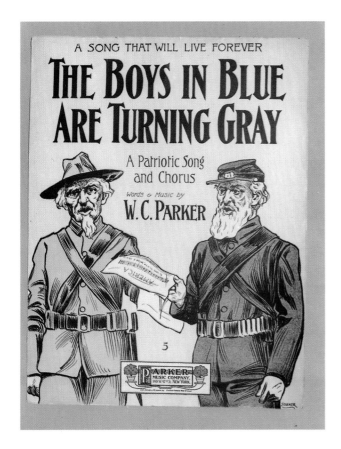

The Boys in Blue Are Turning Gray
"The dove of Peace spreads out her wings," and onetime foes during the Civil War stand side by side on this Starmer cover. (1895)

3. The Spanish-American War— "The Splendid Little War"

In 1898 the United States was drawn into a conflict between Cuba and Spain, despite President McKinley's efforts to avoid war. It was a small, short war compared to the huge World Wars of the twentieth century and was termed "the splendid little war" by Theodore Roosevelt's friend John Hay.

The hostile actions of Spain could no longer be ignored when the United States battleship *Maine* was destroyed in Havana harbor in February by an explosion that took the lives of 266 officers, sailors, and Marines. A naval court of inquiry determined the explosion was caused by a submarine mine, and the war cry "Remember the *Maine*!" was taken up. Spain and the United States went to war, and many songs about the sinking of the *Maine* were written to dramatize the event.

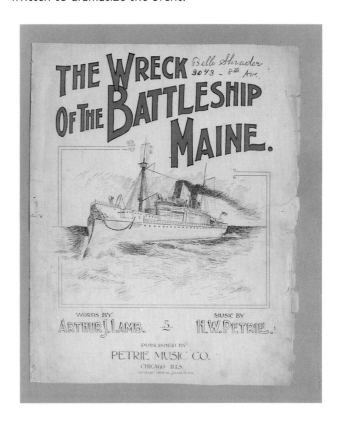

The Wreck of the Battleship Maine
Song pays homage to brave gallant lads in blue who have gone to their last long sleep in the angry deep. Belligerent lyrics added fuel to the national spirit of vengeance. (1898)

"My Sweetheart Went Down With the *Maine*" was dedicated by composer Bert Morgan to a nameless lady who lost her beloved on the ship. The dedication begins with a poignant quotation from Lord Alfred Tennyson: "'Tis better to have loved and lost, Than never to have loved at all." The song then urges, "Rouse ye, my countrymen, rouse, let not his death be in vain. Strike down the cowardly fiends who slaughtered the crew of the *Maine*." This was the clarion call to battle in a war that lasted less than eight months, yet took a toll of over 6,000 American soldiers and sailors who were either killed in battle or died of wounds, or perished from malaria, dysentery, and typhoid.

President William McKinley took up the reins as Commander-in-Chief of the military and brought the war to a quick conclusion. McKinley was a strong President, and the United States became a world power under his leadership—winning the Spanish-American War, occupying Cuba, Puerto Rico, and the Philippines, and annexing Hawaii. He was assassinated by an anarchist during his second term in office, and Vice President Theodore Roosevelt succeeded to the Presidency.

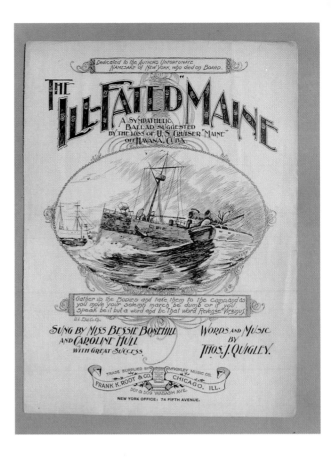

The Ill-Fated Maine
Sad ballad about the loss of life on the *Maine* has inflammatory inscription by Virginus: "Gather up the bodies and take them to the camp, and as you move your solemn march be dumb or if you speak be it but a word and be that word, Revenge." (1898)

My Sweetheart Went Down With the Maine
Bert Morgan composed this sad song of betrothed lovers whose lives were forever changed when the ship sank in Havana harbor. Cover photo shows the *Maine* in her former glory. (1898)

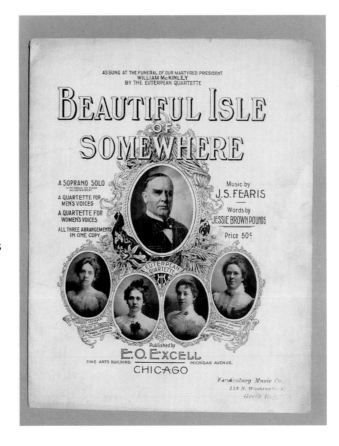

Beautiful Isle of Somewhere
Song was performed by the Euterpean Quartette at the funeral of President William McKinley. (1901)

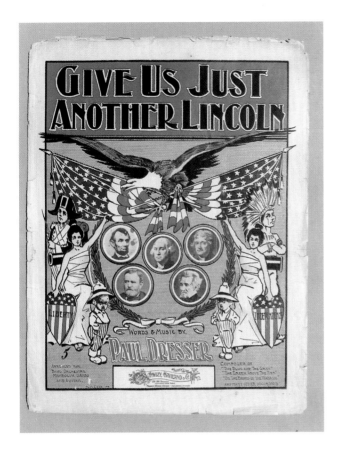

Give Us Just Another Lincoln
This Paul Dresser song came out in election year 1900, and was a plea for sanity and intelligent leadership in the presidency.

Yankee Dewey
Spirited saga of the Battle of Manila Bay is set to the strains of "Yankee Doodle." An imposing photograph of Commodore Dewey graces the cover. (1898)

What Did Dewey Do to Them?
Patriotic tribute to Dewey relates in six verses his triumph at Manila Bay. (1898)

Commodore George Dewey became a hero of the Spanish-American War. As commander of the Asiatic Squadron, he routed the entire Spanish fleet in the Battle of Manila Bay, inspiring a great many songs.

Composer Abe Holzmann was inspired by Dewey's triumph upon the battleship *Olympia* when the brave Captain Gridley was awaiting orders from his superior. "You may fire when you are ready, Gridley!" said Dewey. "Well, boys, let's blaze away!" came the quick rejoinder, and the guns poured their deadly contents into the enemy. As related in the Sunday July 6, 1902 edition of the *New York Herald*,

"Holzmann incorporated into his musical composition the deep meaning of these words. The grumbling of the guns as they poured shot and shell into the vitals of the Spanish fleet, the cry of the sinking foe, the bursting of the shells, the wild wail of anguish and despair from the writhing survivors, commingled with the death dealing projectiles as they flew into the holds and upon the decks of the dismantled battleships, are one and all graphically repeated in melodic structure in 'Blaze Away' by Abe Holzmann."

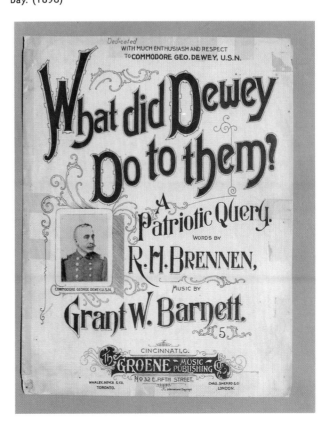

Battle of Manila March and Two Step
This instrumental piece was dedicated to Admiral Dewey, the hero of Manila, by composer Phil B. Perry. (1898)

The Philippines Grand March
Piano piece by J. K. Kyte features a fine photo of an unidentified warship from the Spanish-American War. (1899)

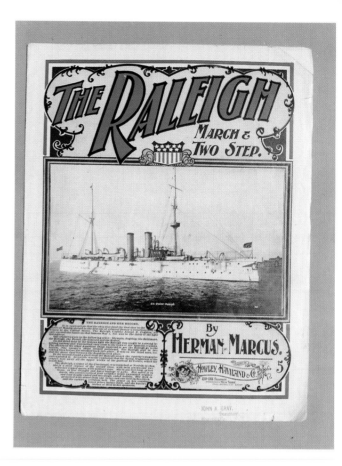

The Raleigh March and Two Step
The U.S. Cruiser *Raleigh* fired the first shot in the battle of Manila, and is honored in this march by Herman Marcus. Her proud record is reported on the cover. (1899)

Blaze Away
Holzmann's inspired march and two-step depicts a charging cavalryman on a spirited horse amidst a barrage of shellbursts. (1901)

In June of 1898 Lieutenant Richmond Pearson Hobson became an American hero when he and a skeleton crew attempted to sink the old collier *Merrimac* in the narrowest part of the channel at Santiago, Cuba, thereby bottling up the entire Spanish Atlantic Fleet. Though the plan went awry and the *Merrimac* went down in the wrong place and Hobson and his crew were captured, his exploits thrilled the country. After a month's confinement by the Spanish, Lieutenant Hobson and his crew were released in a prisoner exchange, and received Congressional thanks and promotions.

General Fitzhugh Lee was consul general at Havana when the war started. During the war he reentered the army as a major-general. His military background served him well. During the Civil War he had been a distinguished cavalry general with the Confederate army, leading the last charge of the Confederates at Farmville, Virginia, in 1865. He was elected governor of Virginia from 1886-1890, then started his tenure in Cuba in 1896 by appointment of President Grover Cleveland. After the Spanish-American War he was made military governor of Havana, and retired as a brigadier general in 1901.

"The Blue and the Gray" was subtitled "A Mother's Gift to Her Country." The poignant lyrics describe a mother's grief at losing two sons in gray at the Civil War battles of Appomattox and Chicamauga, and yet another son in the Spanish-American blue uniform at the battle of Santiago in Cuba.

Cuba Liberty March
Composer Will Hunnewell described this piece as "a march for the people," and dedicated it to General Fitzhugh Lee, consul general at Havana during the war. (1898) *Collection of James Nelson Brown*

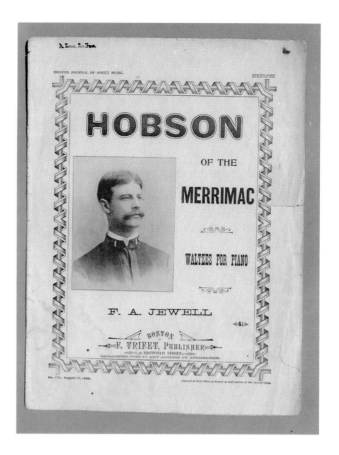

Hobson of the Merrimac
A photo of handsome and courageous Lieutenant Hobson appears on the cover of one of the songs written in his honor. (1898)

The Blue and the Gray
Paul Dresser composed this Spanish-American War tearjerker in 1900. Cover photo of song's interpreter Carrie Fulton.

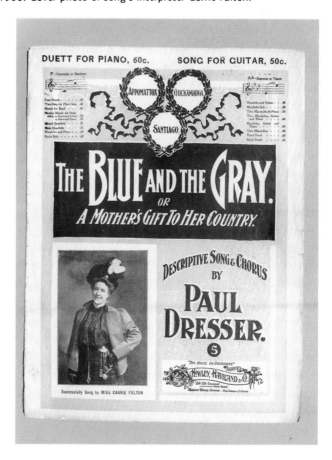

Another sentimental song written in 1901 tells of an old woman bent and gray outside a Southern cottage, bidding her son farewell. Her husband had worn a suit of gray way back in sixty-one, now for the blue she's giving up her joy. The boy had often donned his father's Confederate uniform in childish play, but he laid away the suit of gray to wear the Union blue. He said "We'll show that Dixie's sons will to the flag prove true."

"Break the News to Mother" was written in Charles K. Harris's finest tearjerker style. In the song a young lad in battle is mortally wounded while trying to save the flag from disgrace. A general from afar noted the brave deed and went to the dying youth only to find that it was his own son. The son, with his last breath, sings this sad refrain:

"Just break the news to mother,
She knows how dear I love her,
And tell her not to wait for me,
For I'm not coming home…"

We'll Stand by the Flag
Patriotism was at an all time high in 1898 when E. T. Paull wrote this march with a soldier and sailor on the cover. Lithograph by A. Hoen Company. (WWI reissue)

The Sentinel Asleep
The sounds of war go unheeded by the sentinel standing guard who dozes at his post and dreams of childhood's home. Inset photo of singer E. W. Chipman. (1900)

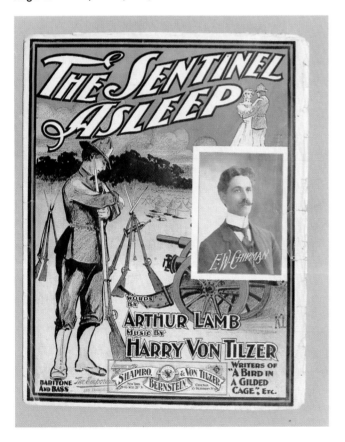

He Laid Away a Suit of Gray to Wear the Union Blue
Edward M. Wickes and Ben Jansen wrote this sentimental and patriotic song in 1901. Inset photos of Mlle. Olivette and Lloyd E. F. Hassmer, performers of the song.

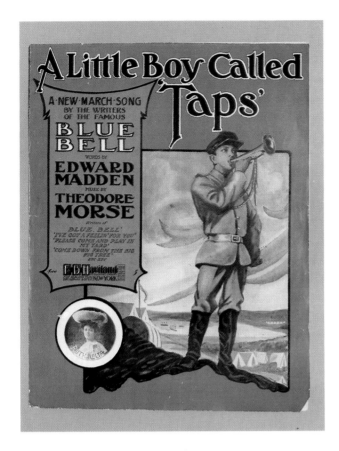

A Little Boy Called "Taps" #1 [red cover]
Madden's lyrics: "From the ranks of death with his parting breath,
Taps is sounding his final call, then is laid to his final rest." Photo of
Ruth Nelta on cover. (1904)

A Little Boy Called "Taps" #2 [blue cover]
Second edition was released by popular demand. Author Edward
Madden notes on cover that he personally knew the mother of the
little bugler "Taps" who lived in a little town in New York. (1904)

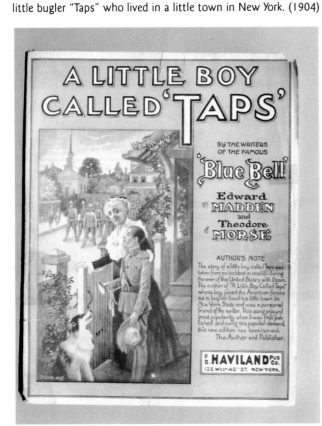

Break the News to Mother
Composer Harris was reportedly besieged with requests for copies of
this song during World War I, and in 1917 reissued it with a
different cover by Starmer. This edition with cover photo of Minnie
Shult is the Spanish-American War issue. (1897)

Only One Lost
A great battle was fought and the victorious troops were overjoyed
at news of only one casualty, but at home a widowed mother wailed
her grief, the one that was lost was her only son. (1901)

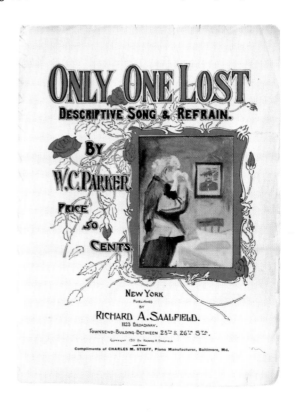

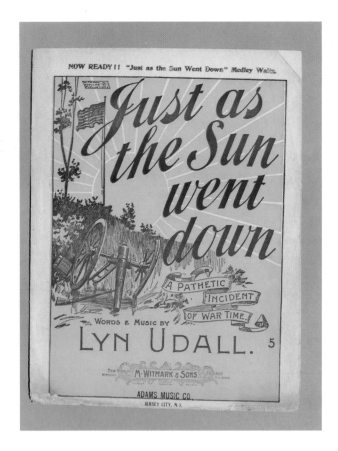

Just as the Sun Went Down
As the sun went down, two soldiers dying on the battlefield each kissed a lock of hair—one, a lock of gray, with thoughts of mother; the other, a lock of brown, with thoughts of his sweetheart. (1898)

One of the saddest songs to come out of the war was "I'll Be There, Mary Dear," a tale of a soldier who leaves his sweetheart behind, promising to meet again 'neath the oak tree after the war. He returns, "a lad with empty sleeve," afraid she will no longer love him with only one arm, and under the old oak tree he finds a silent grave; his sweetheart has passed away, gone from him forever.

Not all the songs from the Spanish-American War were so sad. Bands were playing Sousa's rousing "Stars and Stripes Forever," and the troops were singing "A Hot Time in the Old Town." Reckless reporting by the newspapers of William Randolph Hearst and Joseph Pulitzer stirred the country to battle, and young men rose to the challenge with patriotic fervor.

Theodore Roosevelt was a greatly admired hero of the Spanish-American War. When the war started, Roosevelt resigned his position as Assistant Secretary of the Navy to assist in the organization of the First U. S. Volunteer Cavalry. He succeeded to the command of the regiment and personally led the cavalry division in a bold attack on the Spanish outpost, Kettle Hill, during the battle of San Juan Hill. Criticized by career officers as an impetuous "schoolboy charge," the assault of Roosevelt's Rough Riders, as his troops came to be called, successfully weakened the Spanish position and resolve, and inspired a vast number of popular songs and marches.

I'll Be There Mary Dear
Andrew Sterling and Harry Von Tilzer wrote this sad song in 1902. Inset photo of singer Raymond Teal.

Goodbye Little Girl Goodbye
Will Cobb and Gus Edwards wrote this farewell song. Another soldier falls in battle with the rose his lady love gave him clasped to his heart. Inset photo of singer Albert Tint of the Al Field Minstrel troupe. (1904)

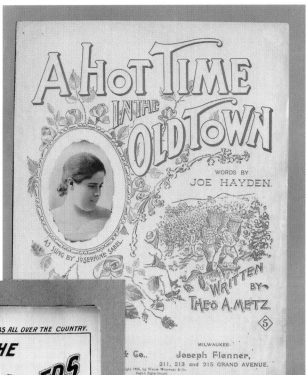

A Hot Time in the Old Town
Song was a favorite of U.S. troops in Cuba and the Philippines, and is connected with the charge of Theodore Roosevelt's Rough Riders up San Juan Hill. (1896)

In the Hills of Old Carolina
Grief-stricken soldier returns from the war to find his sweetheart Elaine, whom he loved so well, passed away and buried in the hills. Photo of song's interpreter Eugene Wiener. (1902)

Stars and Stripes Forever
This 1940 reprint of Sousa's famous march has a magnificent rendering of the flag by distinguished artist Howard Chandler Christy.

Mr. Volunteer
Paul Dresser wrote this song in tribute to the returning soldiers of the Spanish-American War. (1901)

The Charge of the Roosevelt Rough Riders
Several editions of Charles Coleman's march were printed. This 1941 reprint was dedicated to Ex-President Theodore Roosevelt.

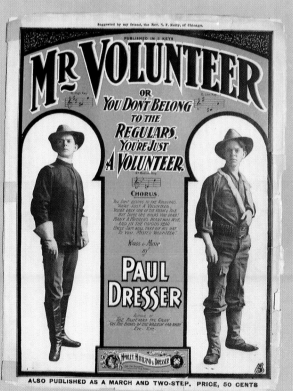

Roosevelt March
Theodore "Teddy" Roosevelt was the leader of the Rough Riders, President of the United States, and the winner of the Nobel Peace prize in 1906. March by F. Carl Jahn was written in his memory in 1919.

As President, Roosevelt became known as "The Peacemaker" and was awarded the Nobel Peace Prize for his diplomacy in mediating the conflict between Russia and Japan in 1904-1905 known as the Russo-Japanese War. The war was fought over control of Manchuria and Korea. The Japanese attacked and blockaded the Russian fleet at Port Arthur in 1904, and after the Russians suffered a series of defeats, the two nations agreed to arbitration in the United States. They met aboard the Presidential Yacht *Mayflower*, with President Roosevelt serving as mediator, and negotiated a peace treaty on September 5, 1905, signed at Portsmouth, New Hampshire, in which Russia ceded lands and holdings to the Japanese.

The Japanese demanded an enormous indemnity from Russia, which Roosevelt refused to approve, and soon thereafter relations between the United States and Japan turned sour. Adding fuel to the simmering resentment of the Japanese people were exclusionary acts that were passed against Japanese immigrants in California. Roosevelt was able to defuse the situation, but felt that in view of this so-called "yellow peril," a strong naval presence in the Pacific would be a sensible move.

Japan's Triumphal March and Two-Step
The Russo-Japanese War ended in 1905 and soon thereafter relations between the United States and Japan became strained. This march was written in 1904.

Roosevelt often quoted an African proverb, "Walk softly and carry a big stick." His "big stick" was the sixteen battleships of the United States Navy. He had them painted white, and inaugurated an around-the-world cruise in 1907 by this "Great White Fleet" to advertise the Navy's strength and the military presence of the United States of America.

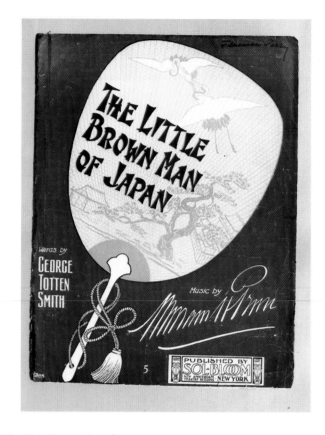

The Little Brown Man of Japan
The bright eyed little brown man of Japan is admired in this song as "the best friend to know, or the bitterest foe," as he fights the "bold Mister Bear" (Russia). Music by William H. Penn, words by George Totten Smith. (1904)

Songs Related to the Great White Fleet

Sailors Welcome
This musical accolade was written to welcome United States sailors of the Great White Fleet to San Francisco. (1908)

Goodbye, Sailor Boy
The many farewells to sailors of the Great White Fleet inspired this song by Lowitz and Stamper. (1906)

March Battleship Connecticut
March and two-step has cover photo of battleship *Connecticut* of the Great White Fleet as she churns through the foamy brine. (1905)

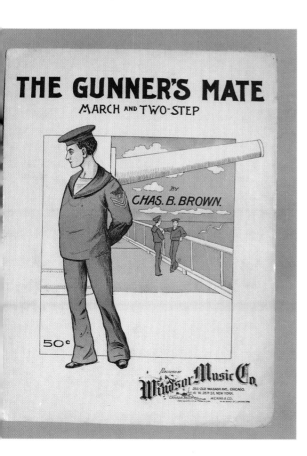

The Gunner's Mate
March and two-step by Charles B. Brown was written in honor of the specialized sailor. (1901)

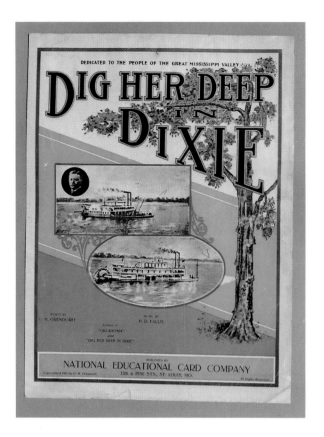

Dig Her Deep in Dixie
Maritime presence at home is evident on song cover with photos of paddle wheeler U.S. *Col. Mackenzie*, sternwheeler U.S. *Illinois*, and a photo inset of Roosevelt. (1907)

Oceana Roll
"Billy McCoy was a musical boy on the cruiser *Alabama*" who played that raggy "piana" to the other sailors. (1911)

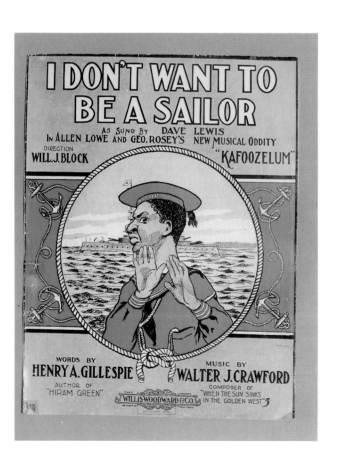

Though not actually a declared war, an altercation between the United States and Mexico in 1914 caused President Woodrow Wilson to send all available warships to Mexican waters in a punitive action for insult to the United States. A battle was fought at Vera Cruz, and many lives were lost. The bandit, Francisco "Pancho" Villa, entered the fray by wantonly killing Americans. An expeditionary force under Brigadier General John J. Pershing was sent in to hunt down Villa, and two skirmishes occurred below the Mexican border that almost led to full-blown war. Peace was eventually established. Another war was looming in Europe, and in 1917 the United States, close to war with Germany, withdrew the troops from Mexico.

I Don't Want to Be a Sailor
Comic song about life in Roosevelt's Navy was written for the show *Kafoozelum*. The lyrics tell of an unhappy Sam Cook who jumped ship to go back to New Orleans. (1905)

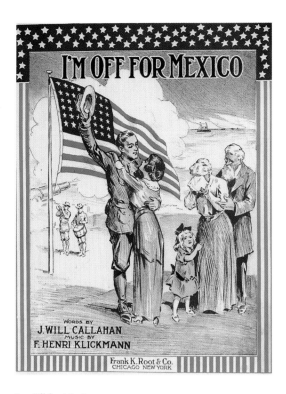

I'm Off for Mexico
Song by F. Henri Klickmann and J. Will Callahan had the strongly worded subtitle "They've insulted dear Old Glory—that means shoot!" (1914)

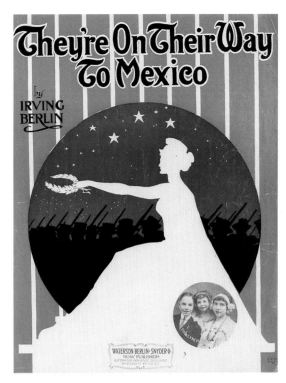

They're On Their Way to Mexico
Irving Berlin wrote this stirring patriotic song about the Mexican war with cover design by John Frew. Inset photo of the Lynch Trio. (1914)

Till We Meet Again
Raymond B. Egan and Richard A. Whiting wrote this deservedly popular song, still a favorite as a farewell song. (1918)

4. World War I

The haunting strains of "Smile the while you wish me sad adieu..." from the World War I song "Till We Meet Again" is a nostalgic reminder of the grim period in American history known as The Great War. More songs came out of this war than the Spanish-American War and World War II combined. They are fine collectibles, and reflect the sentiments of the American people about our country's involvement in the war.

Not only are the music and lyrics interesting, but also are the covers with their pictorial themes of pathos, humor, and patriotism. Marching and fighting soldiers, tearful farewells and flag-waving, and a strong, grim-visaged Uncle Sam are frequent cover subjects. Specific depictions of guns, tanks, ships, planes, and of the real people involved in the fight add greatly to the historical interest of these covers.

The assassination of the Austrian Archduke Franz Ferdinand and his wife in Sarajevo, Bosnia, at the end of June 1914 started what became World War I. Within weeks the British, French, Belgians, Russians, Italians, Serbs, and other Allies were at war with the Germans, Austrians, and Turks. President Woodrow Wilson immediately proclaimed the United States' neutrality, and bewildered Americans with ties to Europe had conflicting loyalties. Many of the early war songs in 1915 took this pacifist approach with themes of anti-war sentiment, but the country was divided, and other pro-war songs took the opposite tack.

You'll Be There
Song by J. Keirn Brennan and Ernest R. Ball reflects pro-war sentiment, "Now the time has come when we must go to war ...ev'ry mother's son, you'll be there!" (1915)

Pacifism or Preparedness?

Don't Take My Darling Boy Away
A mother's plea to the Captain, "You took his father and brothers three, now you come back for more" is the theme of this 1915 antiwar song.

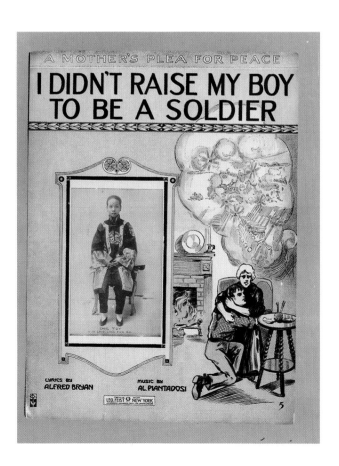

I Didn't Raise My Boy to Be a Soldier
The chorus expresses a protective mother's fear of sending her son off to war. Cover photo of Chee Toy of the Ching Ling Foo Company, ostensibly a performer of the song. (1915).

"I didn't raise my boy to be a soldier,
I brought him up to be my pride and joy,
Who dares to place a musket on his shoulder,
To shoot some other mother's darling boy?"

I Didn't Raise My Boy to Be a Slacker
Vivacious vaudevillian Eva Tanguay promoted this patriotic song praising the young men who fight for liberty. (1917)

"I didn't raise my boy to be a slacker,
I can see him in the thickest of the fray,
A gun upon his shoulder, he's ev'ry inch a soldier,
For his daddy did his bit at Manila Bay."

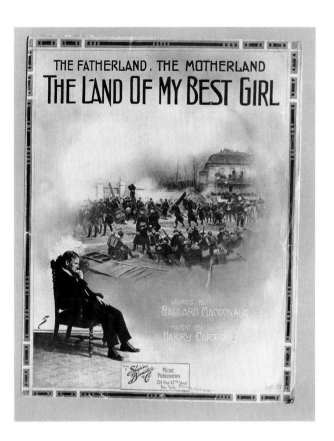

The Land of My Best Girl
The unhappy predicament of a young man of mixed parentage whose father was from Germany, his mother from France, and his best girl from England, is poured out in this ballad. (1914)

The budding movie industry in Hollywood aided in propagandizing the anti-war philosophy with such silent films as *War Brides* (1916). Alla Nazimova portrayed the heroine who had lost all her male relatives at war, and killed herself rather than comply with a government edict to have more children to fight in future wars. Though the setting of the story was in a mythical kingdom, the film effectively preached the pacifist approach to war. When the United States officially declared war in April 1917, pacifism was equated with treason, and all anti-war films including *War Brides* were banned.

Songs were imported from Europe during the early days of the war that created sympathy for the war-torn countries, and helped fuel the fires of pro-war factions in the United States. "Keep the Home Fires Burning" (1915) was a popular sentimental song out of England that imparted a strong message to civilians at home to hide their tears and look for the silver lining till the boys come home. "Pack Up Your Troubles in Your Old Kit Bag and Smile, Smile, Smile," a cheerful song of 1915, was an international hit, sung and whistled by the troops as they marched along.

Widespread outrage was felt in May of 1915 when a German U-boat sank the British luxury liner *Lusitania*. The ship went down in eighteen minutes with a loss of 1,198 lives including 128 Americans. This incident was commemorated in the song "As the *Lusitania* Went Down" with a dramatic cover of a flailing hand reaching up from a raging sea, and a wraith like bride and groom atop a cresting wave.

As the war progressed, American sentiment began turning against the Central Powers when German atrocities in Belgium and their reported use of poison gas at Ypres in 1915 shocked the country. "Belgium Dry Your Tears" came out in 1918 when America finally responded to Belgium's need for help.

President Wilson ran for re-election in 1916, and the presidential campaign was fought mainly over the issue of foreign policy. The country rallied behind Wilson, and support for him was evident in popular songs of the day.

Songs espousing U. S. involvement in the war flooded the market. Feelings ran strong both pro and con, and dramatic garish sheet music covers and patriotic warmongering lyrics fomented guilty feelings and pride of country.

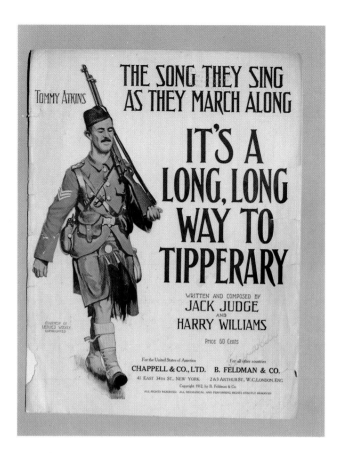

It's a Long, Long Way to Tipperary
This jaunty song, published before World War I, became popular after the war's onset. Cover drawing (courtesy of *Leslie's Weekly* magazine) shows a British sergeant in kilts shouldering an Enfield rifle, the standard piece for the British soldier in World War I. (1912)

War Brides
Silent movie with pacifist story line has cover photo of actress Alla Nazimova emoting her heart out. (1916)

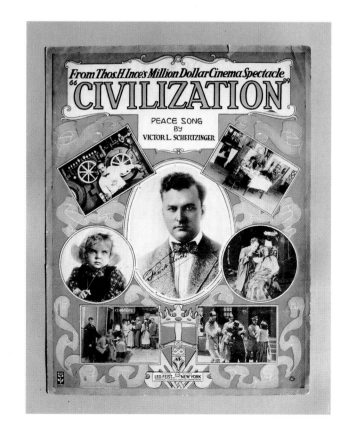

Civilization Peace Song
Thomas Ince produced this monumental silent movie preaching against the wastefulness of war in 1916.

They All Sang Annie Laurie
Soldiers around the camp fire, fearful of the bugle's last call, dreamed of home while singing the sweet strains of Annie Laurie, "the song that reaches ev'ry heart." (1915)

War Babies
Cover photo of frightened children in a war-torn village adds to the pathos of Al Jolson's hit song from his Winter Garden show. (1916)

As the Lusitania Went Down
The poignant subtitle reads, "He thought of the girl who loved him; He thought of their wedding day." (1915)

Belgium, Dry Your Tears
"You've shown us grit and brav'ry, Land of heroes staunch and true, We'll soon be marching side of you" are lyrics by Arthur Freed to Al Piantadosi's music. (1918)

Roses of Picardy
Picardy was a region in northern France often in the news, and the symbolism of a rose dying in Picardy touched hearts around the world. (1916)

95

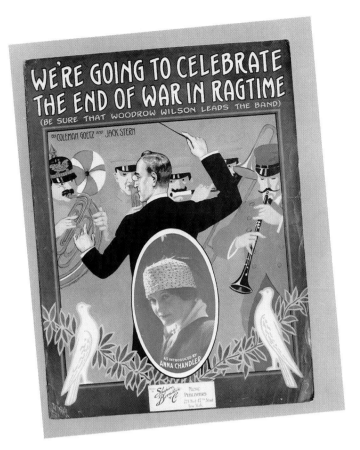

We're Going to Celebrate the End of War in Ragtime
Woodrow Wilson is leading the band on the cover of this pacifist song endorsing neutrality— England, France, Germany, and Italy all at peace. Song was introduced by Anna Chandler. (1915)

Never Swap Horses When You're Crossing a Stream
1916 election year slogan is set to music by Jesse Winne with words by Harold Robe. Cover portrait shows President Woodrow Wilson who was elected to a second term.

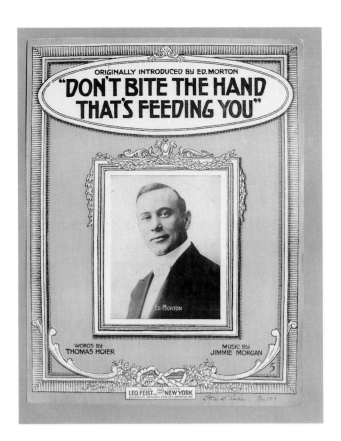

Don't Bite the Hand That's Feeding You
Blunt rhetoric in this 1915 song chides newcomers to America, "If you don't like your Uncle Sammy, then go back to your home o'er the sea …Don't act like the cur in the story, don't bite the hand that's feeding you!" Originally introduced by cover star Ed Morton. (1915)

Answer Mr. Wilson's Call
A clarion call to arms is the theme of this patriotic song of 1917.

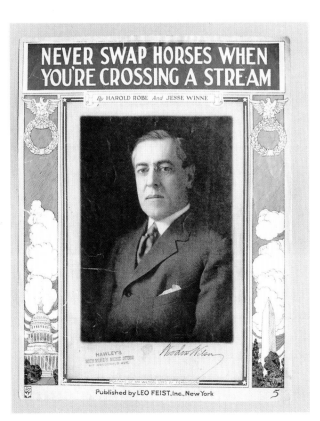

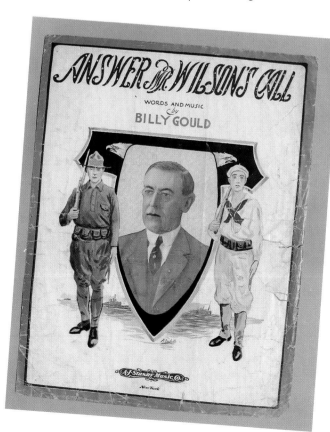

Pro-War Songs

What Kind of an American Are You?
Strong appeal to patriotism comes across with this probing question, "If the Star Spangled Banner don't make you stand and cheer, then what are you doing over here?" (1917)

America, Here's My Boy
Lyrics appeal to the mothers of America, "America, I raised a boy for you, my hope, my pride and joy, but if I had another, he would march beside his brother, America, here's my boy." (1917)

It's Time for Every Boy to Be a Soldier
"Boys of America, get ready. It's time to shout those noble words of Lincoln, 'That the nation of the people, by the people, for the people shall not perish from the earth.'" (1917)

Wake Up, America!
George Graff's eloquent lyrics asked the questions all America was asking, "Are we prepared to give our lives for our sweethearts and our wives? Are our mothers and our homes worth fighting for?" (1916)

Let's All Be Americans Now
Song by Irving Berlin, Edgar Leslie, and George Meyer appeals to all Americans to unite as one, despite their ties to England, France, or Germany. (1917)

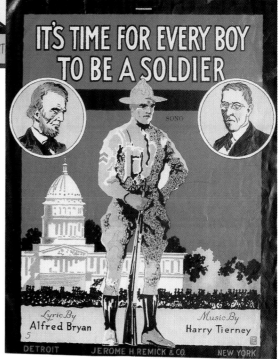

America, He's for You!
Story of a mother who has three sons fighting in the war and "a baby in the cradle and as soon as he is able, America, he's for you." Dedicated by composer Andrew B. Sterling to Privates James and Raymond Sterling U.S.A. (1918)

After German submarines torpedoed three American ships in March 1917, the United States officially declared war on Germany, and the country began mobilizing its resources. The spirit of patriotism was growing, and the number of volunteers in the regular Army, Navy and National Guard increased to 900,000 by September 1917. This still wasn't enough, and Congress passed a conscription act that required all men between the ages of 21 and 30 to register for the draft, from which enough would be drawn to bring the army of the United States up to two million men.

Mississippi Volunteers
Comic song about the Mississippi Volunteers parade, and a Pullman porter down in Comp'ny C who complains, "This life ain't what they cracked it up to be!" (1917)

Over the Top with Your Uncle Sam
"Somewhere in France they are waiting for you to show what the brave Yankee Doodle will do," are lyrics in this martial song. (1918)

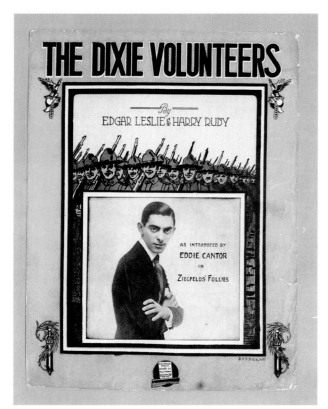

THE DIXIE VOLUNTEERS

By
EDGAR LESLIE & HARRY RUBY

AS INTRODUCED BY
EDDIE CANTOR
IN
ZIEGFELDS FOLLIES

The Dixie Volunteers
Eddie Cantor sang this in Ziegfeld's *Follies*, "Peaceful sons have shouldered guns, their regimental band is playing tunes from Dixieland, the Dixie volunteers are proud to go to war." (1917)

Songs About Women in World War I

Those that were left behind wanted to help the war effort, and mothers and sweethearts were knitting mufflers, socks, and balaclava helmets of khaki wool and grey for the boys over there. Other women did more than just sit home and knit during those trying times. The Red Cross nurse was revered for her bravery at the front. The Salvation Army lassies also helped at the front running canteens, making apple pies for the boys, and creating a little touch of home, endearing the organization and the courageous women in their modest blue bonnets to the U. S. public.

Each Stitch Is A Thought Of You, Dear

WORDS BY
AL SWEET
MUSIC BY
BILLY BASKETTE

LEO. FEIST NEW YORK

Each Stitch Is a Thought of You, Dear
Song was dedicated to that Army of Noble Women—mothers, wives, sisters, and sweethearts—who are doing their bit for the boys over there. (1918)

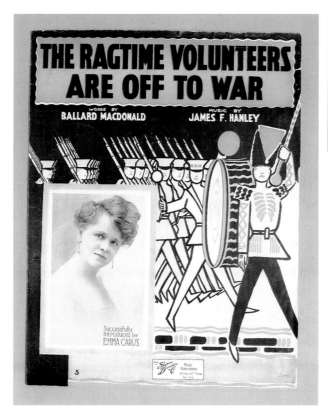

THE RAGTIME VOLUNTEERS ARE OFF TO WAR

WORDS BY
BALLARD MACDONALD
MUSIC BY
JAMES F. HANLEY

Successfully Introduced by
EMMA CARUS

The Ragtime Volunteers Are Off to War
Emma Carus presented this song with a blues twang and a ragtime beat about those darkies lifting their feet as they march off to war. (1917)

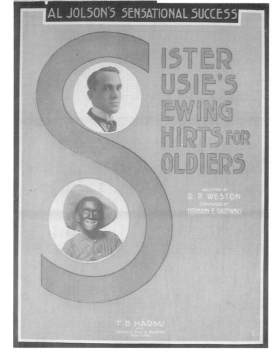

AL JOLSON'S SENSATIONAL SUCCESS

SISTER SUSIE'S SEWING SHIRTS FOR SOLDIERS

WRITTEN BY
R. P. WESTON
COMPOSED BY
HERMANN E. DAREWSKI

Sister Susie's Sewing Shirts for Soldiers
Humorous tongue-twisting song was a huge success for singer Al Jolson in 1914.

There's an Angel Missing from Heaven

There's an Angel Missing from Heaven
The esteem with which the Red Cross nurse was regarded is evident in this touching song about the brave angel of mercy. "Dedicated to the American Red Cross." (1918)

The displaying of a service flag in the window originated during World War I. In 1917 Captain Robert B. Quiesser designed a flag with a red border and a white center with two blue stars, one for each of his sons. He created this symbol so a mother could show "her son was serving the country rather than have her feel an emptiness about the house which would depress her."

The flag had neither presidential nor congressional sanction, but was so widely used that in 1918 the Department of the Army gave it semiofficial recognition and encouraged flying it. Recommendations were that a blue star represent those serving in the U. S. armed forces; a silver star for those wounded or invalided home from overseas, with a gold star superimposed for those who died as a result of such wounds or disease, and a gold star alone for those killed in action. It wasn't until World War II that President Franklin Roosevelt signed a bill approving official designs for the service flag and service lapel button, based for the most part on the earlier design.

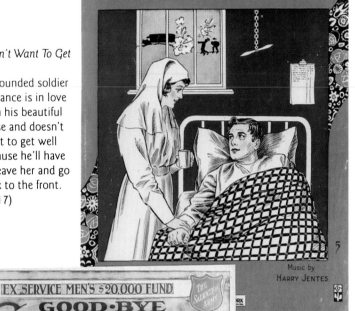

I Don't Want To Get Well
A wounded soldier in France is in love with his beautiful nurse and doesn't want to get well because he'll have to leave her and go back to the front. (1917)

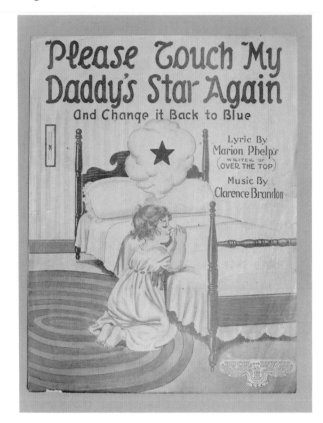

Please Touch My Daddy's Star Again
A dimpled baby prays that the angels will change her daddy's star from gold to blue. (1918)

Goodbye Sally
The nickname "Sally" was given to the popular Salvation Army lassie. The Starmer cover features a photograph taken in France of a Salvation Army post with a uniformed lassie greeting a Yankee soldier. (1919)

THERE'S A SERVICE FLAG FLYING AT OUR HOUSE

There's a Service Flag Flying at Our House
The service flag is proudly hung by father and mother telling of their support and sacrifice during the war. (1917)

Anti-Kaiser Songs

More aggressive sentiments were expressed in an outpouring of belligerent anti-Kaiser and anti-Germany songs. Even little school children were heard paraphrasing the lyrics to "Kaiser Bill":

*"Kaiser Bill went up the hill
to take a look at France;
Kaiser Bill came down the hill
with bullets in his pants..."*

We're All Going Calling on the Kaiser
Rousing song by Jack Caddigan and James Brennan wants Kaiser Willie dead with a lily on his chest. (1918)

WHEN A BLUE SERVICE STAR TURNS TO GOLD

When a Blue Service Star Turns to Gold
Tender sad song about young life that's given in battle, and the grief that is left behind. (1918)

Stars of Honor *March Song*

Stars of Honor
Touching song is dedicated to the Disabled Veterans of World War I, Post 1 in Los Angeles who received the bronze, silver, and gold stars for their sacrifice. (1921)

When the Kaiser Does the Goose-Step to a Good Old American Rag
This comic song envisions the Kaiser goose-stepping endlessly to jazz, the fox-trot, and "The Stars and Stripes Forever" played by Sousa's band. (1917)

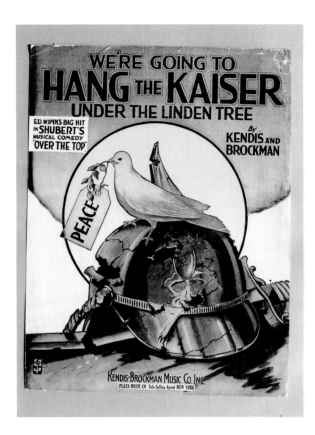

We're Going to Hang the Kaiser Under the Linden Tree
Sung by Ed Wynn in the musical comedy *Over the Top*, this comedy song suggests another way to take care of the Kaiser. (1917)

We'll Knock the Heligo into Heligo Out of Heligoland
Heligoland was a strongly fortified island guarding the entrance to the Kiel Canal, the most important German Naval Base. Caricature cover drawing shows American fleet chasing Kaiser Bill. Inset photo of Collins and Harlen. (1917)

Who Put the "Germ" in Germany
Ragtime novelty song about a professor in Germany inspecting bugs who suggests, "Mr. Edison, please make some medicine to knock the Kaiser into eternity." (1917)

We Don't Want the Bacon, What We Want Is a Piece of the Rhine
Humorous lyrics used a play on words to convey its message, "We'll crown Bill the Kaiser with a bottle of Budweiser." (1918)

Sentimental tearful ballads about mother, sweetheart, and home were rampant during World War I. Songs of farewell, the heartbreak of separation, letters from the battlefield, and pensive children who didn't really understand why Daddy was away spawned many heartrending songs.

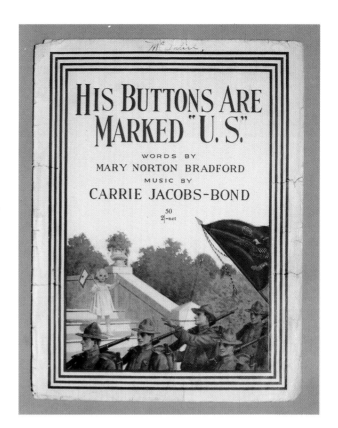

His Buttons Are Marked U.S.
"Though Daddy now wears a brown suit and a gold eagle, his buttons are marked U.S. that spells 'us,' meaning mother dear and me." Lyrics are by Mary Norton Bradford to music by Carrie Jacobs Bond. (1918)

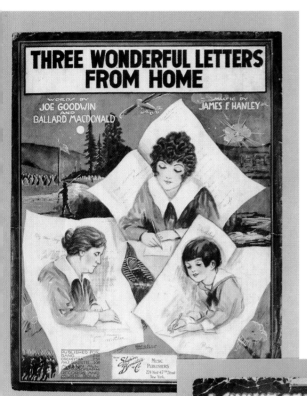

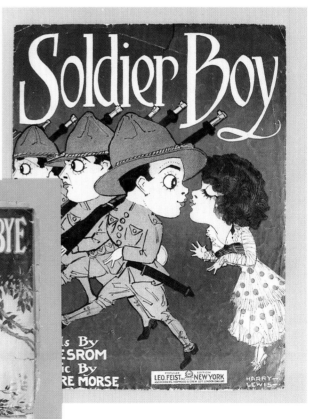

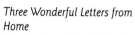

Three Wonderful Letters from Home
Popular hit of World War I about mother, wife, and child writing letters to the soldier in a distant war-torn land. (1918)

I Cannot Bear to Say Goodbye
Tattered sheet music is mute testimony of constant playing, a sad farewell song by soldier to his sweetheart. (1918)

Soldier Boy
Theodore Morse song has eye-catching caricature cover by Harry Lewis. (1915)

That's a Mother's Liberty Loan Greater Vitagraph silent stars, handsome Edward Earle and perennial "mother" Mary Maurice pose on cover of this song about a mother who loans her son to the war effort. (1917)

I Miss Daddy's Goodnight Kiss
With sweet baby sighs and tear-dimmed eyes, her little heart is yearning for Daddy. (1918)

So Long, Mother
Al Jolson never failed to bring a lump to the throat when he sang this famous mother song. (1917)

Just a Letter for a Boy Over There from a Grey-Haired Mother Over Here
A letter from mother has "a kiss inside and words of cheer to hide that way down in her heart there's a tear." Cover star Frankie La Brack sang this song. (1918)

Just a Baby's Letter Found in No Man's Land
A battle-weary soldier finds a letter lying on the ground filled with crosses for baby kisses and just four tender words, "I love you, Daddy." (1918)

The beautiful song "Smiles" was a sentimental favorite all through the war, becoming a standard of World War I. Lee Roberts reportedly wrote the tune on the back of a cigarette package, and J. Will Callahan's inspired lyrics were a perfect addition. "Somewhere In France Is the Lily" was another popular hit of World War I composed by Joe Howard.

The lighter side of war was expressed in humorous songs. The country needed a laugh now and then, as did the servicemen, and Tin Pan Alley was there to provide it. "Long Boy (Good-bye, Ma! Good-bye, Pa! Good-bye, Mule)" told of "a long, lean country gink from 'way out West where th' hop-toads wink" who joined up and went away to war saying goodbye to his mule "with yer old hee-haw."

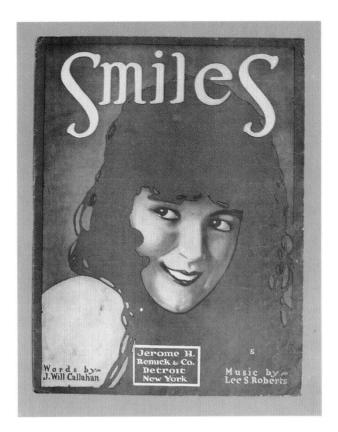

Smiles
Popular hit of World War I has slogan inside the cover "Every vegetable on the table means a Hun on the run." (1918)

Humorous Songs of World War I

K-K-K-Katy
The soldiers and sailors loved to sing this sensational stammering song by Geoffrey O'Hara— a major hit at home as well. (1918)

Somewhere in France Is the Lily
Song was published with two different covers; this, and another with a large photo of composer Joseph Howard. (1917)

"*Somewhere in France is the Lily,*
Close by, the English Rose;
A Thistle so keen, and a
Shamrock green, And each loyal
flower that grows..."

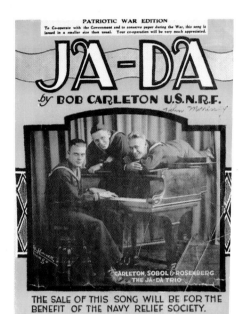

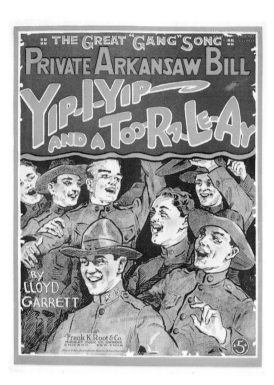

Ja-Da
The nonsense syllables caught on, and this raggy song by U. S. sailor Bob Carleton became a major hit. Composer is seen here with the Ja-Da Trio. (1918)

Would You Rather Be a Colonel with an Eagle on Your Shoulder or a Private with a Chicken on Your Knee
Eddie Cantor performed this comic song in Ziegfeld's *Follies*. This smaller format is the new patriotic war size designed to save paper—approximately 7" x 10" instead of the normal 11" x 14". (1918)

Private Arkansaw Bill
Everybody's looking for poor old Bill for starting that song "Yip-i-yip and a Too-ra-le-ay"…a hundred fellows have said they'd kill the poor devil. (1918)

If He Can Fight Like He Can Love Good Night, Germany!
This racy number was also published in the small format. "If he's just half as good in a trench as he was in the park on a bench, then ev'ry Hun had better run!" Inset photo of singer Ray Samuels. (1918)

Irving Berlin made many humorous contributions to the music of World War I. He was drafted into the army during the spring of 1918, and the songs continued to pour from his prolific pen. While stationed at Camp Upton in Yaphank, Long Island, his commanding officer asked Berlin to do a show to raise money for a base community house. Berlin complied, happy to do so as one of the perks was being able to keep some decent hours and not get up at five a.m. to the sound of the detested bugler. He wrote the music for the show *Yip-Yip-Yaphank*, which was touted as a "musical mess cooked up by the boys of Camp Upton with words and music by Sergeant Irving Berlin."

The famous bugle song "Oh! How I Hate to Get Up in the Morning" was largely autobiographical, as the thing he hated most about Army life was reveille. He dedicated it "To my friend Private Howard Friend who occupies the cot next to mine and feels as I do about the bugler." He wasn't happy with another song he wrote for the show, describing it as "just a little sticky, I couldn't visualize soldiers marching to it" and moth-balled it until 1939 when Kate Smith introduced it on her CBS radio show to phenomenal success. The song was "God Bless America."

Berlin replaced "God Bless America" with the show's concluding song,"We're On Our Way to France" with 277 soldiers wearing full battle gear marching from the stage through the aisles of the theater out the doors as if they were leaving for the battlefields. In fact, in the last performance of the show in the dramatic finale, the soldiers did indeed march to a troop carrier that left for France.

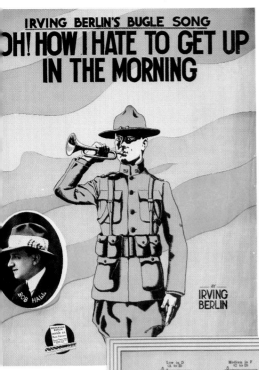

IRVING BERLIN'S BUGLE SONG
OH! HOW I HATE TO GET UP IN THE MORNING
BY IRVING BERLIN

BOB HALL

Oh! How I Hate to Get Up in the Morning
Private Irving Berlin was one of the hits of the show when he performed this in his Army revue *Yip, Yip, Yaphank*. Bob Hall's photo on cover. (1918)

The show played for thirty-two performances at the Century Theater in New York, then successfully toured Boston, Philadelphia, and Washington, D. C. The base community center to be built at Camp Upton with the proceeds of the show was never constructed as the war ended in November and there was no longer a need for it.

They Were All Out of Step But Jim
A proud mother watching her son on parade in his uniform and gun made the observation that they were all out of step but her son Jim. Cover photo features Yvette and Sarnoff. (1918)

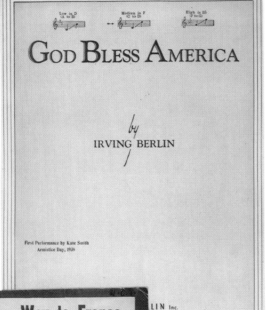

GOD BLESS AMERICA
by
IRVING BERLIN

First Performance by Kate Smith
Armistice Day, 1938

God Bless America
Irving Berlin's timeless song was introduced on Armistice Day 1938 by Kate Smith who sang it with characteristic vigor throughout World War II.

Goodbye France
Sergeant Berlin wrote this tribute to France, "We were glad to stand side by side with you, mighty proud to have died with you, you'll never be forgotten by the U.S.A." (1918)

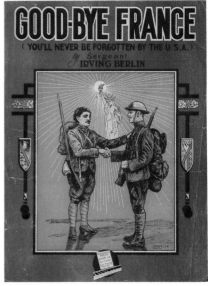

GOOD-BYE FRANCE
(YOU'LL NEVER BE FORGOTTEN BY THE U.S.A.)
By Sergeant IRVING BERLIN

We're On Our Way to France

YIP-YIP-YAPHANK
A MILITARY MUSICAL "MESS" COOKED UP BY THE BOYS of CAMP UPTON
WORDS AND MUSIC BY SERGEANT IRVING BERLIN
STAGED BY PRIVATE WM. SMITH

We're On Our Way to France
This rousing number from *Yip, Yip, Yaphank* has a dramatic cover by Barbelle appropriately colored in khaki on white. (1918)

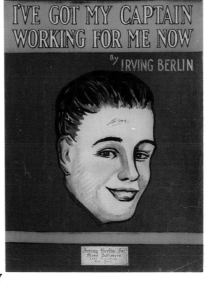

I'VE GOT MY CAPTAIN WORKING FOR ME NOW
By IRVING BERLIN

I've Got My Captain Working for Me Now
After the war, Berlin wrote this humorous song about a guy who hires his old Captain as a clerk in his father's factory "...he calls me, 'Sir'...revenge is sweet." (1919)

Many songs espoused the upbeat sentiment of "Let's win the war," and the greatest of them all was "Over There." George M. Cohan wrote the stirring patriotic song in 1917, and it was published in several editions, the most famous being the Norman Rockwell painting of soldiers bivouacking around a campfire. The song was first sung to an enthusiastic crowd at a Red Cross benefit in New York's Hippodrome Theater by Charles King, but was given a bigger boost by popular Nora Bayes who successfully introduced the song in her show. The Bayes' edition, published by William Jerome Publishing Corporation, is thought to be the earliest (although a brown, black, and tan cover with a photo of Harry Ellis put out by the same publisher is said to exist).

"Over There" was a huge success, selling records and sheet music in the millions. The song had a big revival in World War II. The 1942 Warner Brothers movie *Yankee Doodle Dandy*, a superb biographical film based on the life of George M. Cohan featured some of Cohan's most popular songs, including a rousing production number of "Over There." James Cagney starred as Cohan, and his dynamic portrayal won for him the Academy Award for best actor in 1942. The song subsequently was admitted to the Hall of Fame as a prime example of American patriotic music, and brought great honors to its composer.

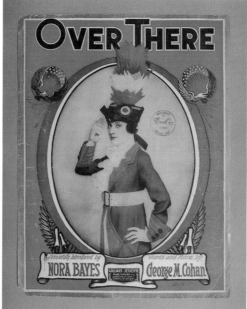

Over There (Nora Bayes)
Probable first edition has cover photo of Nora Bayes in military dress. (1917)

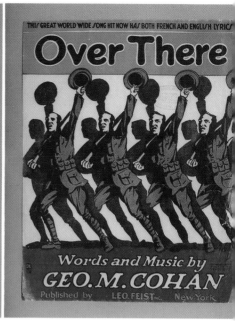

Over There (Henry Hutt drawing of soldiers)
Dramatic cover is based on sketches by Henry Hutt of a spotlighted chorus line of strutting soldiers with shouldered rifles and outstretched arms flourishing their hats. (1917)

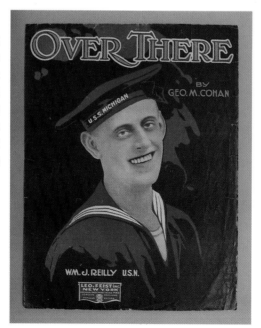

Over There (Sailor Reilly)
This common variety pictures the sailor, William J. Reilly, from the USS *Michigan*. This is the same Reilly seen on covers of "What'll We Do With Him Boys?" and "When the 'Yanks' Come Marching Home." (1917)

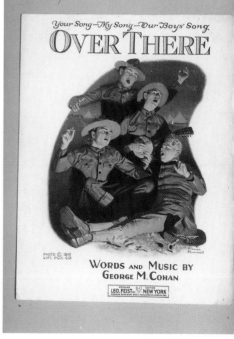

Over There (Rockwell cover)
This most famous and coveted edition has cover by Norman Rockwell. (1917)

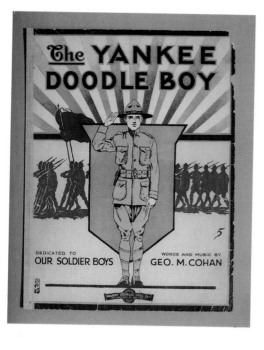

The Yankee Doodle Boy
This is a World War I reprint of George M. Cohan's 1904 song from the Broadway show *Little Johnny Jones*. (1915)

The Navy Will Bring Them Back
Lively song promises that the Navy who took the soldiers overseas are ready to bring them back home as heroes in victory. (1918)

When You Come Back
George M. Cohan's photo and facsimile autograph adorn the cover of this optimistic song. (1918)

Forty-Five Minutes from Broadway
When James Cagney accepted the Oscar for his role in *Yankee Doodle Dandy* he concluded his remarks with Cohan's famous line, "My mother thanks you, my father thanks you, my sister thanks you, and I thank you." (1943)

U. S. naval history is well represented on World War I covers. The battleship USS *Oklahoma* (BB37) was commissioned in 1916, and after fitting out and completing trial runs and maneuvers, she was assigned to Battleship Division Six, U. S. Atlantic Fleet. In August 1918 she departed Hampton Roads, Virginia, for European waters, and was based at Berehaven, Bantry Bay, Ireland, during the remainder of the war. Her primary duty was to protect convoys from possible German raiders.

After the Armistice was signed on 11 November 1918, *Oklahoma*, with units of both Divisions Six and Nine, steamed triumphantly into New York the day after Christmas. The cover picture on the historical song sheet "The Navy Will Bring Them Back" was probably taken that day. F. Muller took the photograph of the battleship with officers in the foreground, sailors covering the deck, sailors perched on the big guns and the open lattice mast, and sailors on the two side boat cranes.

This is the same ship that was later torpedoed by the Japanese in their attack on Pearl Harbor on December 7, 1941. She overturned, with a number of men trapped beneath the upturned hull. An heroic civilian employee, Julio De Castro, heard a tapping sound from the capsized ship, and with a group of workers, managed to cut through the hull until all known survivors were released. Of the 82 officers and 1,272 men aboard *Oklahoma*, 20 officers and 395 men were either killed or missing.

The ship's charred hulk was later raised, but it never again rejoined the fleet. After being used in atomic bomb tests at Bikini Atoll in June 1946, the ship was sold for scrap. While being towed from Pearl Harbor to San Francisco, she parted the tow line and plunged three miles to the bottom of the sea. The vessel went down as a proud ship should, rather than be turned into an ignominious pile of scrap metal.

Navy Songs from World War I

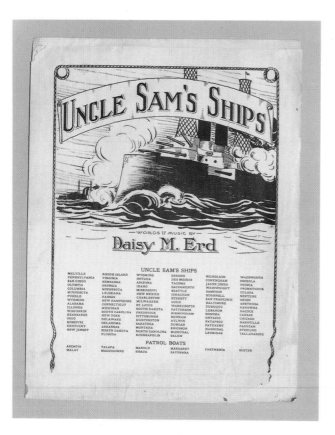

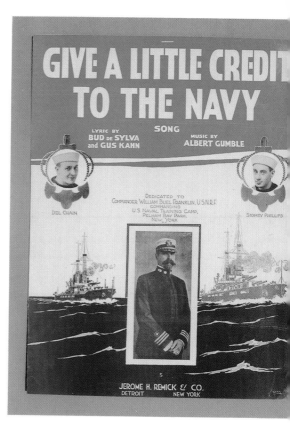

Give a Little Credit to the Navy
"We took the boys across without a single loss, trick'd the submarines with ease, and as the U-boat sank into the sea, the soldiers cheer'd and sang out joyfully." Dedicated to Commander William Buel Franklin, Commanding Officer of the U. S. Naval Training Camp at Pelham Bay Park, N.Y. (1918)

Uncle Sam's Ships
An interesting Navy-related song by Daisy M. Pratt Erd, Chief Yeoman U.S.N.R.F., has a cover drawing of a battleship, and a list of Uncle Sam's Ships in World War I. (1917)

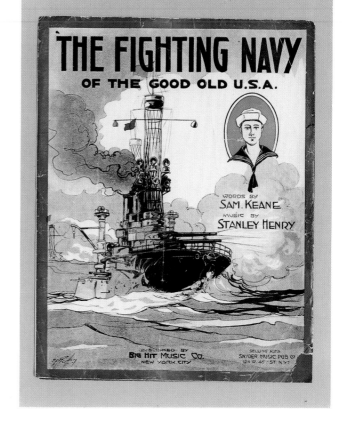

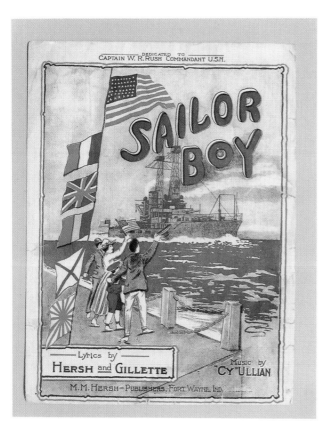

The Fighting Navy (Of the Good Old U.S.A.)
Song honoring the Navy is illustrated by E. H. Pfeiffer with a dramatic drawing of a warship firing her big guns. (1917)

Sailor Boy
This tribute to U. S. sailors has a special dedication to Captain W. R. Rush, Commandant U.S.N. (1917)

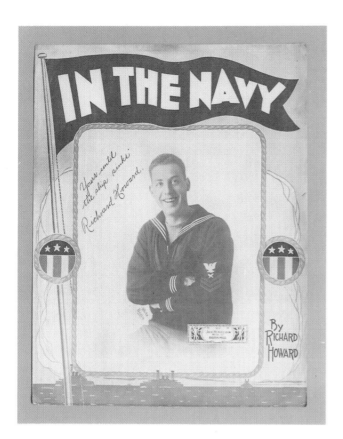

In the Navy
First Class Petty Officer composer Richard Howard enjoyed his stint in the Navy during World War I and wrote this rousing song, "It's the finest kind of life I ever knew." (1918)

Pick a Little Four Leaf Clover
A soldier boy asks his sweetheart to send him a four leaf clover to bring him luck. Sung by the Great Lakes Sextette with Sousa's Great Lakes Band. (1918)

Strike Up the Band Here Comes a Sailor
Originally copyrighted in 1900, this attractive edition with a cover illustration by Pfeiffer is a reprint of a popular song from the Spanish-American War. (1918)

Old Glory Goes Marching On
Exciting Navy piece features ten thousand American bluejackets on the cover. They have formed a living flag on the grounds of the United States Naval Training Station at Great Lakes, Illinois, and are standing at salute. (1918)

Songs with Battle Scenes on Cover

Part of the mobilization plan was to not only send great numbers of American infantrymen and artillerymen to the Western front, but also great fleets of aeroplanes to wreak havoc on the Germans. Though Americans had invented the aeroplane, the war department had done little in forming an aerial service, and much precious time was lost in formulating plans, designing and building planes, and training workmen and aviators. Aeroplanes in the early days of the war were used chiefly to reconnoiter, and were valuable for spotting the fire of artillery, for dropping bombs on strategic objectives, and for photographing the enemy's works.

I'll Be Over Your Way in the Mornin' Bill
Song tells of Paddy McTwist who enlisted as an aviator and wrote this letter to old Kaiser Bill, "I'm bringin' a present for you that is grand, a beautiful lily to hold in your hand." Barbelle cover shows World War I biplane. (1918)

The Yanks Are At It Again
"You'll find them ev'rywhere, on land and sea and in the air." Fine cover by E. E. Walton shows the various services of the United States military in action. (1918)

Just as the Sun Went Down
This reissue of the Spanish-American War song has a new cover designed by Dunk of New York, showing barbed wire trenches, machine guns, planes, and a tank. (1918)

On the Land, On the Sea, In the Air (We'll Be There)
Rousing march song has a Starmer cover showing a battle raging on land, sea, and in the air. (1917)

If I'm Not at the Roll Call (Kiss Mother Goodbye for Me)
Soldiers burrowed in trenches that were fortified by tangles of barbed-wire, hiding so completely they were often only a few hundred yards from their foes without knowing it. The soldier in this song asks his friend to notify his mother if he doesn't make it. (1918)

Let's Keep the Glow in Old Glory
Grim angry Yanks protecting mother, child, and flag are marching into battle on this evocative patriotic piece. (1918)

We're Coming Back to California
This historical piece was dedicated to Colonel Thornwell Mullally. The little bears on the cover are symbolic of California's "Bear State" moniker. Official song was approved by Major General Strong seen in cover photo. (1918)

The Sunshine Division
Photo of "Sunshine Division" is on back cover of "We're Coming Back to California." First units embarked for overseas in August 1918, and were ordered to La Guerche (Cher) as replacements for combat divisions at the front. (1918)

Many songs were written in honor of specific persons or military regiments and are of special historical value. Those with photographs of the actual participants are especially valuable to families of the men. "We're Coming Back to California" was the U.S. Government Official Song of the 40th (Sunshine) Division of Camp Kearny, California. The front cover features a picture of Major General Strong who commanded the division from the time of its organization, and the back cover has a wonderful wide lens photograph of the marching soldiers of the Sunshine Division.

Back in the Old Town Tonight
Cover has photo inset of Colonel Clarence S. Wadsworth, and is dedicated to "Company L. of the 12th Regiment, N.G.N.Y." The New York National Guard was the nucleus of the 27th Division which fought in the front line attack on Vierstandt Ridge, and also saw action near Bony in 1918. (1916)

101st Regiment, U.S.A. March
The 101st Regiment was known as "Boston's Own," a part of the 26th Division who fought in France. (1917)

It's a Long Way to Berlin, But We'll Get There
March song was dedicated to Lieutenants Joseph E. Barrell and Eugene J. Orsenigo of the 71st New York Infantry, part of the 27th Division. Singer Flora Stern on cover. (1917)

The Khaki Boys of the U.S.A.
Song is dedicated to the 104th Regiment of the U.S. Infantry, part of the 26th Division known as the "Yankee Division" because its units were made up from the National Guard troops of the New England States. They fought in France at the second Battle of the Marne, at St. Mihiel, and at Verdun. (1917)

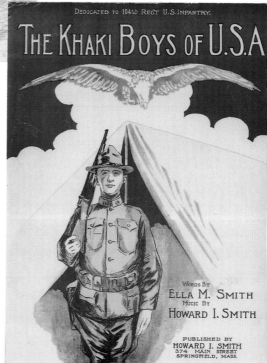

U.S. Spells Us
Marine privates William C. Wilson and Harold Johnston wrote this song in honor of the Marine Corps, and dedicated it to Colonel and Mrs. Lincoln Karmany of Mare Island, California. The Marines in France were part of the Second Division who fought bravely in the battle at Belleau Wood. (1918)

Are We Downhearted? No! No! No!
A large cover photo of about three dozen happy-looking soldiers, one of them holding a dog, is credited to International Film Service. Little is known of the jolly group, "The Shrapnel Dodgers, the Sensation of Vaudeville." (1917)

General John J. Pershing graduated from West Point in 1886 and had a brilliant career in the Army. He fought the Apaches with the 6th Cavalry in Arizona, and was in charge of the Indian scouts during an uprising of the Sioux in Dakota. He served in Cuba during the Santiago campaign in 1898, and commanded the expedition into Mexico against Pancho Villa in 1916. His successful military career was clouded by the great tragedy in his personal life when he lost his wife and three small daughters in a fire at the Presidio in San Francisco. Only his five-year old son was saved. During World War I Pershing created almost from nothing the vast structure of the American Expeditionary Force in Europe.

Mobilization! Pershing's goal was to build an American force in France numbering a million men, and by July 1, 1918, he met his goal. The Americans distinguished themselves on the battlefields of France, and as news reached home, new songs flooded the market. Written in tribute to the valiant heroes, some were in a serious vein, others took a decided humorous twist.

I'll See You Later, Yankee Land
Cover photo on Charles K. Harris song shows elated troops on a ship transport on their way to France. (1917)

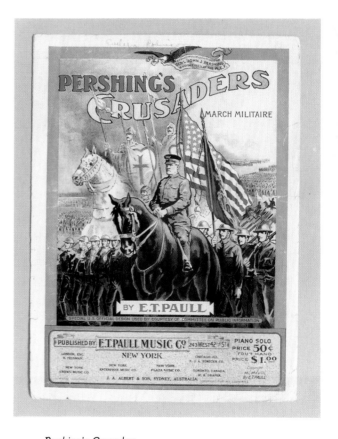

Pershing's Crusaders
E. T. Paull march is inscribed to General Pershing and the men of the A.E.F. Chromolithograph cover was created by A. Hoen Company of Richmond, Virginia, using an official U.S. design courtesy of Committee on Public Information. (1918)

We Don't Know Where We're Going But We're On Our Way
Dedicated to Colonel Dan Moriarty and his Gallant Regiment, the "Fighting Seventh" Illinois Infantry, part of the 33rd Division known as the "Prairie Division." They distinguished themselves in the Meuse-Argonne offensive operating with the 17th French Army Corps, taking about 650 prisoners. (1917)

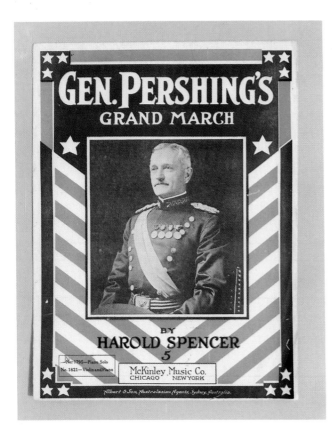

General Pershing's Grand March
March by Harold Spencer has photo of Pershing in full dress uniform wearing some of his large medals. (1918)

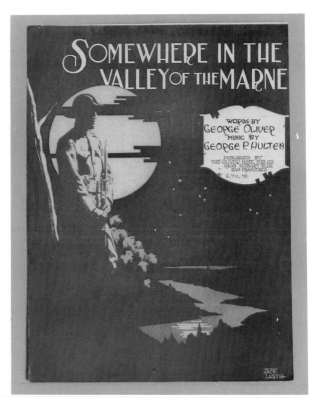

Somewhere in the Valley of the Marne
In this song, thoughts are with the loved one across the ocean "where the shrieking shot and shell have shattered ev'ry brooklet in the valley of the Marne River." (1918)

I'm Hitting the Trail To Normandy
Normandy is the region in northern France along the English Channel where the first American soldiers were deployed. Inset photo of Artie Mehlinger. (1917)

Goodbye Broadway, Hello France
Imaginative cover drawing shows General Pershing shaking hands with General Ferdinand Foch, the Commander-in-Chief of the Allies in France. (1917)

116

Au Revoir, But Not Goodbye
Simple lovely melody by Albert Von Tilzer has touching words by Lew Brown in this tender goodbye song. (1917)

When Alexander Takes His Ragtime Band to France
American ragtime hits France during World War I: "Those ragtime tunes will put the Germans in a trance, they'll throw their guns away and start right in to dance." Sung by cover star Belle Baker. (1918)

Hinky Dinky Parlay Voo
The composer of this tune is unknown, but it was widely sung in Europe during the war, and had many new verses added as it passed from troop to troop. This collection of twenty-two verses was compiled in 1924. Billy Glason on cover.

Lorraine, My Beautiful Alsace Lorraine
A French soldier dreams of the village steeple, and the quaint old fashioned people of his home in Alsace Lorraine. (1917)

When Yankee Doodle Learns to Parlez Vous Francais
Speaking the language of love in France was top priority for the lonesome serviceman in this song by Will Hart and Ed Nelson. Inset photo of "Janet of France." (1917)

Songs from Other Lands

Soldiers in far-off foreign lands succumbed to the charms of native girls in Europe and even in Hawaii. "Aloha Soldier Boy" finds a native Hawaiian girl in Waikiki bidding farewell to her soldier boyfriend long before Hawaii became a state. "When We Wind Up the Watch on the Rhine" has an imaginative cover by Pfeiffer of a soldier and his girl sitting atop a huge pocket watch, a clever takeoff on the word "watch" in the title. As the war exacerbated, all the great powers of Europe and eventually most of the countries of the world were involved.

Aloha, Soldier Boy
Lovers in Waikiki are parted by the war, and the soldier is cautioned by his sweetheart to stay away from "little, naughty, Frenchy maidens." (1918)

There's a Green Hill Out in Flanders
Flanders, a section of Belgium that included parts of France and the Netherlands, was the scene of many bloody battles. In this song, a brave soldier dies for his country and is buried on a green hill in Flanders. Photo of performers Burns and Fabrito. (1917)

The Russians Were Rushin', the Yanks Started Yankin'
This song tells it all. "The Russians were rushin' the Prussians, the Balkans were balkin', Turkey was squawkin', Rasputin disputin', and Italy scootin', the British were skittish, Canadians raidin', Frenchmen invadin', the Bulgars were bulgin' the Belgians, and the Yanks started yankin'. (1918)

When We Wind Up the Watch on the Rhine
Imaginative cover by artist Pfeiffer depicts young couple sitting atop a huge pocket watch. (1917)

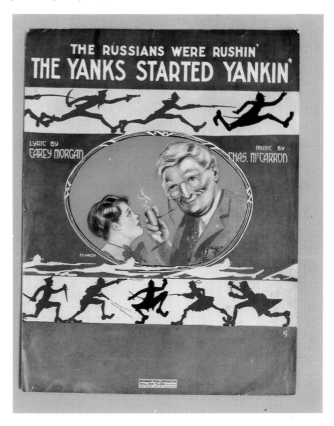

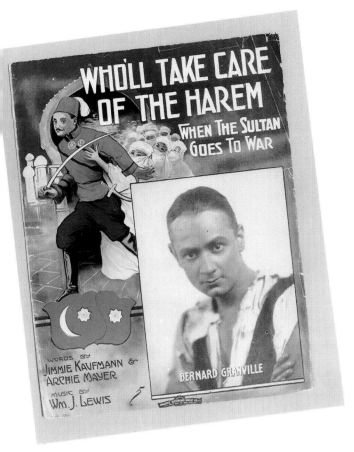

Who'll Take Care of the Harem When the Sultan Goes to War
Comic song was written about Turkey being late entering the war because the Sultan didn't want to leave his harem! Inset photo of Bernard Granville. (1915)

Won't You Say a Word for Ireland?
This song sends a plea to President Wilson to remember the brave Irish-Americans in the peace negotiations, and put in a good word for Ireland. (1917)

Wartime personalities from foreign lands were also honored on sheet music. The French Army under Marshal Ferdinand Foch distinguished themselves in the first Battle of the Marne, and in March 1918 the Allies appointed him Commander-in-Chief for all their armies. He was known as a man of thought as well as action, his maxims being "A battle won is a battle in which one will not acknowledge oneself beaten," and "Victory goes always to those who deserve it by the greater force of will..."

Sir Douglas Haig, Field Marshal and Commander-in-Chief of the British forces in France in 1915-1918, was honored with the 1918 song "Marshal Haig." After a distinguished military career, Haig devoted himself to the welfare of ex-servicemen. He is credited with the creation of Poppy Day on November 11th, with the proceeds from the sale of poppies for the benefit of ex-servicemen.

Marshal Petain, a popular French hero during World War I, was known as "the savior of Verdun" for his tough leadership during Verdun's defense in 1916. He was responsible for pushing the Germans back to the Ardennes. He is shown on the cover of the march "Commander-in-Chief." His days of glory ended after World War II when he was condemned by the provisional government under General Charles de Gaulle for betrayal of French national interests while acting as premier of the Vichy government.

Cover illustrations of World War I weapons abound, but most of them are generic, rather than specific, types. American doughboys in battle dress, with full field packs, gas masks, cartridge belts, rifles and bayonets, and "teapot" steel helmets are often portrayed on battle covers.

Commander-in-Chief
March and two-step by F. H. Losey honors the great French Marshal Ferdinand Foch. (1918)

Songs Covers with Weapons and Uniforms of World War I

Till Over the Top We Go
Soldier with automatic rifle charges into battle on cover of Democratic State Committe campaign song. Back cover explains the party platform, and has photos of President Wilson with local politicians urging "Elect a 100% War Congress next fall." (1918)

America First
Military uniforms are featured on the cover of this call to arms that hearkens the youth of the country to stand and fight. (1917)

Every Boy's a Hero in This War Today
Good illustration of a battle scene with tanks and machine guns. (1918)

Over the Rhine
Striking Starmer cover shows biplanes flying over a pontoon bridge, over which soldiers, tanks, cannons, and a Red Cross truck are crossing. In the distance a burning enemy encampment sends clouds of smoke into a battle-scarred sky. (1917)

The Berlin Special
A 1903 Springfield rifle with fixed bayonet is accurately drawn by Jack Lustig on the front cover of this song. (1918)

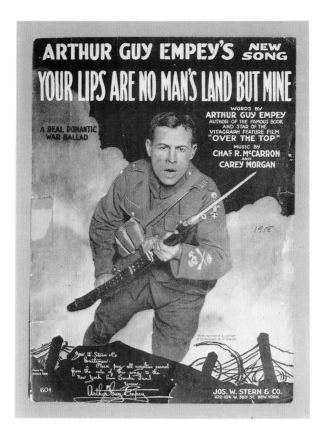

Your Lips Are No Man's Land But Mine
Arthur Guy Empey is seen on the cover of this song from his Vitagraph movie feature *Over the Top*. (1918)

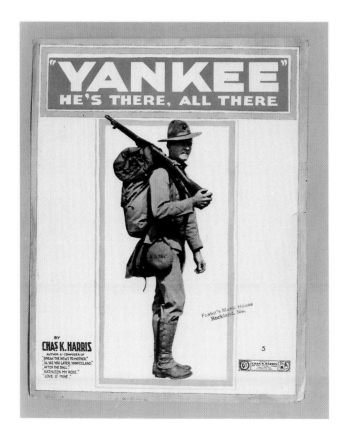

Yankee, He's There, All There
Photograph of a soldier in battle dress is seen on the cover of this World War I song by Charles K. Harris. (1917)

When the United States went to war in April 1917 President Woodrow Wilson appointed Herbert Hoover as special wartime food administrator in charge of production, conservation, and distribution of food for the public, the military forces, and the Allies. Wartime food rationing went into effect on a voluntary basis, and meatless, wheatless, and porkless days were observed to conserve food for the armed forces. American families were urged by the government to plant backyard gardens. Fuel conservation was encouraged with gasless Sundays and coalless Mondays to help save fuel resources. People tightened their belts, and Hoover's food administration was an effective part of the war effort at home and in Europe.

I Thank You, Mr. Hoover
Songwriter Clarence Gaskill wrote this comedy song about all the sacrifices a hen-pecked husband had to make to aid the conservation war effort as outlined by wartime food administrator Herbert Hoover. (1918)

American families were urged by the government to plant backyard gardens. The back cover of "The Man Behind the Hammer and the Plow" has a proclamation by President Woodrow Wilson to the People dated April 16, 1917, from the White House. It is an impassioned appeal for the nation to come together during the wartime emergency, particularly the farmers of the country. Slogans like "Win the war with bread and lead" reflected the conservation push, and were sometimes found along the inside spine of sheet music from the period.

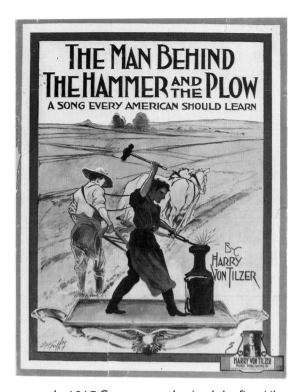

The Man Behind the Hammer and the Plow
Harry Von Tilzer's lyrics pay tribute to those who stayed behind, to the builders of the nation—mechanics, engineers, and farmers, and the men who till the soil. (1917)

For Your Boy and My Boy
Gus Kahn wrote these lyrics to Egbert Van Alstyne's rousing martial music, "Buy bonds for your boy and mine." The back cover puts it eloquently, "The safest investment in the World—a Liberty Bond! If you can't jab a bayonet, grab a bond!" (1918)

In 1917 Congress authorized the first Liberty Loan and War Savings Certificates to meet the expenses of war, and a nationwide drive swung into action. Celebrities like Douglas Fairbanks from the world of movies, and Madame Ernestine Schumann-Heink from the world of opera sold bonds, and President Woodrow Wilson himself made a pitch for Liberty bonds at a Broadway show. School children across the country did their part by pasting 25-cent Liberty stamps into books to help the effort, goaded on by the slogan, "Lick a Stamp and Lick the Kaiser!"

Before the war commercial sheet music was printed in the folio or large size (11" x 14"). In 1915 publisher Leo Feist advertised a new style of sheet music on the back covers of some of his songs. The big innovation was the printing of a song on two pages with no loose insert page. He wrote: "No embarrassing pauses while pianist struggles with loose or missing leaves—or, as very often happens, comes to a dead stop while some kind friend picks the loose sheet from the floor."

The idea was further expanded during the war by a reduction in the size of the music to a smaller format with no insert page. This 7" x 10" small format music was printed on an experimental basis, ostensibly to save paper during the war. It was in use for only a short time, mainly in 1918 and 1919. Some of these songs were also printed in the large size.

After the war, publishers didn't return to the old large size music, but standardized their music to the 9" x 12" size we know today. Feist called his smaller song sheets War Editions and explained, "To Cooperate with the Government and to conserve paper during the War, this song is issued in a smaller size than usual. Save! Save! Save is the watchword today. This is the spirit in which we are working and your cooperation will be very much appreciated. Leo. Feist, Inc."

A Soldier's Dream
Famous singer Madame Schumann-Heink cancelled her professional engagements for one year to sell war bonds, and to tour the camps and cheer up the boys, among whom were four of her own. (1918)

Small Format World War I Songs

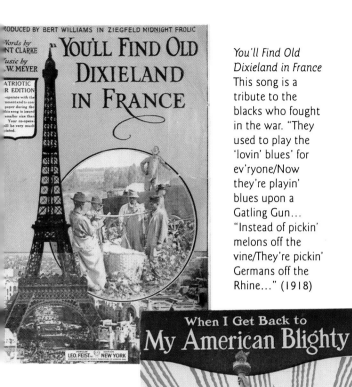

You'll Find Old Dixieland in France
This song is a tribute to the blacks who fought in the war. "They used to play the 'lovin' blues' for ev'ryone/Now they're playin' blues upon a Gatling Gun... "Instead of pickin' melons off the vine/They're pickin' Germans off the Rhine..." (1918)

My American Blighty
An English Tommy tells a Yank, "Why, Blighty, lad, means home, sweet home, and Ma and Dad, and wife and kiddies and all you had that you loved and left behind." (1918)

I Ain't Got Weary Yet
Johnny Dunn who sailed away to fight the Hun sang these words, "...was wounded in this fight, shot at sunrise, gassed at night, outside of that I feel all right." (1918)

Singing was encouraged by the government as a morale booster during the war, and pocket size song folios were freely distributed by the Committee for Public Information to patrons at local theaters and to the soldiers and sailors. Some of the folio titles were "Songs the Soldiers and Sailors Sing" and "Liberty Songs."

The folio "Songs of Cheer" was praised by the *Saturday Evening Post*. "Here are the songs our boys sing when they march away—the choruses they sing in trench and dugout over there—the songs they'll sing when they come marching home from victory." The cover blurb suggested sending it to a boy or a friend in France. "It will cheer him up and do more to make him happy than almost anything you can give him. Uncle Sam's is a singing army—and 'Songs of Cheer' is just what his battling nephews want— a handy, practical book of the songs they love to sing."

The Armstice ending the war was signed November 11, 1918, and a joyful country welcomed home the war weary servicemen. Boatload after boatload of men arrived, greeted by bands and ticker-tape parades, and the proud faces of loved ones shedding tears of joy and relief. The war was finally over and the country was at peace.

Songs the Soldiers and Sailors Sing
The power of song as a morale booster was recognized by the Leo Feist publishing company, and this pocket-size folio of songs sold for fifteen cents in 1918.

Homecoming Songs

How 'Ya Gonna Keep 'Em Down on the Farm
Big post-war comic hit song asks the pertinent question about a returning soldier who has seen the gaiety of Paris. (1919)

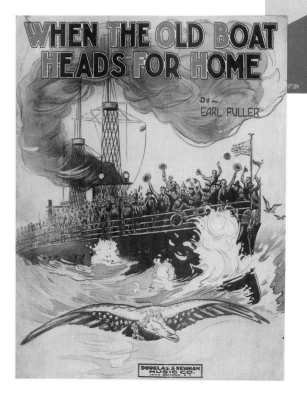

When the Boys Come Home
John Hay, Secretary of State during the Civil War, wrote these lyrics while he was private secretary to President Lincoln. The joy of homecoming is set to spirited music by Oley Speaks. Cover by distinguished illustrator Raeburn Van Buren. (1917)

Give a Job to the Gob and the Doughboy
Adjustment to civilian life is a trying time for the war veteran, and this song urges more than just welcome—give him a job! (1919)

He's Had No Lovin' for a Long Long Time
"Hide away the service flag you waved for him, give him all the kisses that you've saved for him…" (1919)

When the Old Boat Heads for Home
"Hats in the air, yelling 'Hip, Hip, Hooray!'…never again will we roam" are joyful lyrics in this 1918 song.

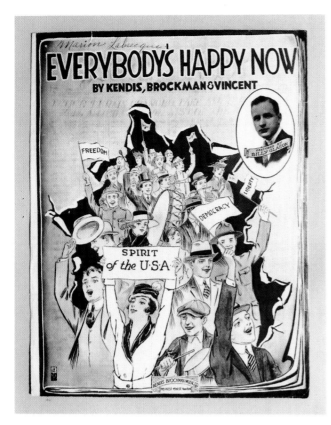

Everybody's Happy Now
"From coast to coast there's a great big celebration... it's all over, and everybody's happy now." (1918)

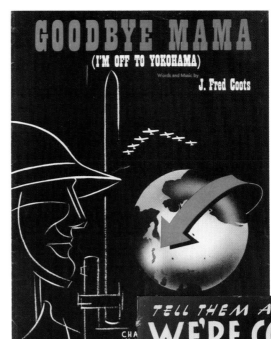

Goodbye Mama (I'm Off to Yokohama)
A young soldier sang this song as he marched off to war, "We'll soon have all those Japs right down on their 'Japa-knees'." (1941)

Tell Them All in Tokio We're Coming
"Our guns and shells have red hot things to say...in Tokio, Berlin, and Naples" are words to this fight song. (1942)

5. World War II

Without warning, Japanese warplanes bombed the port of Pearl Harbor near Honolulu, Hawaii, on December 7, 1941. The country was stunned by the heinous attack and by the terrible losses incurred, and immediately declared war on Japan.

One of the first battles of the war was fought at Wake Island, an atoll in the central Pacific belonging to the United States. It was a strategically important refueling stop for the Navy, and was being developed into an air and submarine base when it came under aerial bombardment from the Japanese a few hours after the strike at Pearl Harbor. A small marine detachment held off the first Japanese landing attempt, but on December 23, the Japanese returned with reinforcements and succeeded in taking the island from the greatly outnumbered U.S. force, and held it until 1945. The fall of Wake Island and Guam effectively cut off the U.S. supply line between Hawaii and the Philippines.

Tora! Tora! Tora!
Extraordinary action cover depicts the Japanese attack at Pearl Harbor. Artist Robert McCall was commissioned by 20th Century-Fox to do an on-location painting of the capsized and burning ships on Battleship Row under attack by Mitsubishi "Zero" fighter planes and Aichi "Val" dive bombers. (1970)

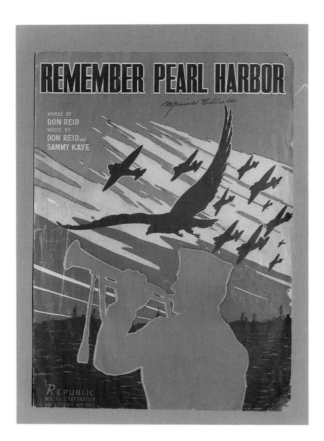

Remember Pearl Harbor
One of the first songs to come out of World War II was a spirited march that rallied the country to fight the foe. (1941)

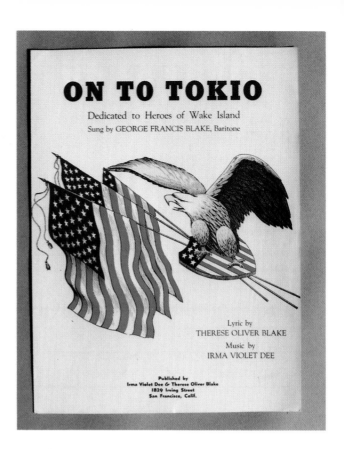

On to Tokio
This U.S. Marine fighting song was dedicated to the heroes of Wake Island. (1942)

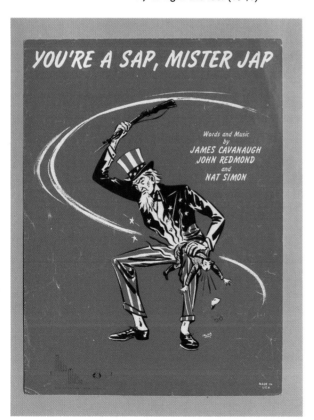

You're a Sap, Mister Jap
Anti-Japanese sentiment lashed out from this slangy 1941 song with a cover drawing by Im-Ho of an irate Uncle Sam spanking a Japanese soldier. (1941)

War was already under way in Europe when the United States entered the fight. Earlier in 1941 President Roosevelt had supported the British with the Lend-Lease Act which made American war materials available to the Allies. Now Germany, Italy, and Japan banded together as the Axis powers and declared war on the United States. The conflict exploded into World War II, and the country geared up for war. The peace that followed World War I was short-lived; less than twenty-five years had elapsed and now the United States was again at war.

The first peacetime selective service act took effect in 1940, and young men with low draft numbers were sent to U. S. bases for one year's training. These optimistic young recruits sang songs like "Goodbye Dear I'll Be Back In a Year," until war was declared and military service became a serious business. Concerned young men and women then voluntarily entered the services in unprecedented numbers.

Patriotism was at an all time high, and the country was united as never before in its effort to win the war. Those who couldn't fight worked in defense plants to produce much-needed planes, tanks, ships, and guns, and these civilian workers—both male and female—were glorified in song.

Adolf
A British chap takes Adolf Hitler over his knee on this cover designed in England by Laurence Wright. (1939) *Collection of James Nelson Brown*

Who Do You Think We Are?
The Axis powers, Hitler, Hirohito, and Mussolini, are characterized in this song, "You Adolf mustache, the Devil's best match... you silly Mikado, the Holy desperado... You bulky Il Duchi, just full of spaguchi... Who do you think we are?" (1943)

Defend Your Country
Patriotic song was inspired by the Army poster, "Defend Your Country," painted by Major Tom B. Woodburn, U.S.A. Quote on the back cover is by George Washington, "To be prepared for war is one of the most effectual means of preserving peace." (1940)

Goodbye Dear I'll Be Back in a Year
Optimistic draftee sings, "They took my number out of a hat...but when I get back we'll buy that cottage just outside of town." Ronnie Kemper, singer with Horace Heidt's band, is featured on cover. (1940)

Be a Hero, My Boy
Pictorial cover by R. Fabri shows a battle scene of a Japanese Zero blowing up, a Japanese ship taking a hit, and a German tank on fire while American forces are victorious. (1943)

127

Milkman, Keep Those Bottles Quiet
This blues rhythm song from the Metro-Goldwyn-Mayer movie *Broadway Rhythm* is the lament of a swing shift defense worker who sleeps during the day and works at night. Ginny Simms and Tommy Dorsey on cover. (1944)

He's 1-A in the Army and He's A-1 in My Heart
Encouraging song praises the physically fit young man who is classified 1-A for service in the military. (1941)

Don't Talk
Factory workers were warned to beware of spies overhearing national security secrets, "…Zipper up your lip, 'cause loose talk may sink a ship, …button your trap 'cause loose talk may help the Jap…" (1943) *Collection of James Nelson Brown*

The Song of the Shipyards
Todd Shipyards Corporation, one of the world's ranking ship construction, repair, and conversion companies during World War II, gave out these complimentary copies. Cover shows a Victory merchant ship under construction. (1942)

Rosie the Riveter
Rhythmic song praises patriotic Rosie, smeared with oil and grease, who works on the assembly line on the riveting machine producing the B-19, working for victory. (1942)

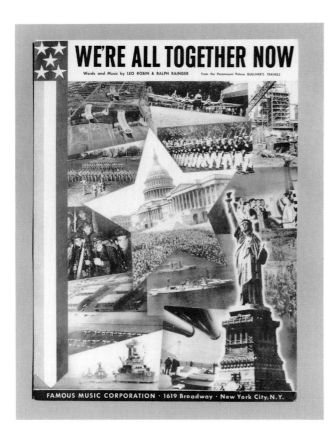

We're All Together Now
Song written in 1939 for the movie *Gulliver's Travels*, took on a new meaning as the country mobilized for war. Cover shows inductees, marching servicemen, battleships, airplanes, a shipyard and landing field—all presided over by a glowing Statue of Liberty.

As in World War I, patriotism was equated with buying War Bonds. Many World War II song sheets have the familiar "V for Victory" symbol with a minuteman poised at the ready and the message: "Buy War Bonds and Stamps for Victory." Celebrities from all walks of life were involved in the sale of war bonds.

Carole Lombard, a beautiful Hollywood actress at the peak of her career, was killed in a plane crash in 1942 while returning to California from a bond selling tour of the Midwest. President and Mrs. Roosevelt sent a telegram to her bereaved husband, Clark Gable, expressing their condolences.

"Mrs. Roosevelt and I are deeply distressed. Carole was our friend, our guest in happier days. She brought great joy to all who knew her and to millions who knew her only as a great artist. She gave unselfishly of her time and talent to serve her government in peace and war. She loved her country. She is and always will be a star, one we shall never forget nor cease to be grateful to. Deepest sympathy."

Irving Berlin was again involved in fund-raising for the war effort. He wrote many songs with revenues donated to worthy causes and organizations—the Red Cross, the Army Ordnance Department, and Navy Relief.

True Confession
President Franklin D. Roosevelt awarded actress Carole Lombard a medal as "The first woman to be killed in action in the defense of her country in its war against the Axis powers." She is seen here with actor Fred MacMurray on cover of theme song from 1937 Paramount movie.

Until that Rising Sun Is Down
Defense bond campaign song was dedicated to General Douglas MacArthur. Lyrics go, "…Every bond that we buy pulls a Jap down from the sky." (1942)

In 1942 Irving Berlin wrote and produced *This Is the Army*, an all-soldier show patterned after his World War I success *Yip-Yip-Yaphank*. A big hit from this show was a revival of "Oh, How I Hate To Get Up in the Morning" performed by Berlin himself in his old World War I uniform. The popular stage show was eventually made into a Warner Brothers movie, *This Is the Army*, starring young actor Lieutenant Ronald Reagan, future President of the United States. The Army Emergency Relief Fund received all the net proceeds from the sale of this music.

Winged Victory, a musical show written by Moss Hart, was produced by the Army Air Force in 1943. Commanding General H. H. Arnold wrote about the musical play: "It is an expression of the spirit of our men wherever they may be—in a bomber high over Germany, on a landing strip in New Guinea—or even here behind the footlights…"

Irving Berlin also wrote the theme song for The National Defense Savings Program, "Any Bonds Today?" Copyrighted by Secretary of the Treasury Henry Morgenthau, Jr., it was printed by the U.S. Government Printing Office, and designated as a souvenir copy, not to be sold. Morgenthau also published "Ev'rybody Ev'ry Payday" urging regular investments in war bonds and stamps.

There Are No Wings on a Fox-Hole
Irving Berlin's affection for the men of the infantry is evident in this stirring song written in their honor. (1943)

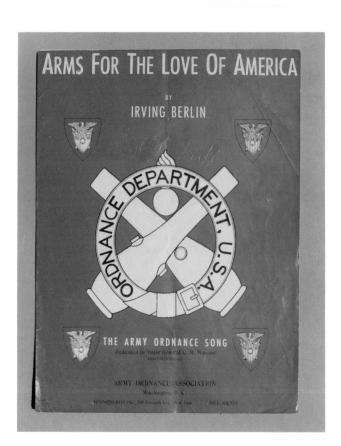

Arms for the Love of America
Irving Berlin dedicated this tribute to Major General C. M. Wesson, Chief of Ordnance, who averred in his address on Army Arsenal Day in 1941, "We must be prepared and we shall be prepared!" (1941)

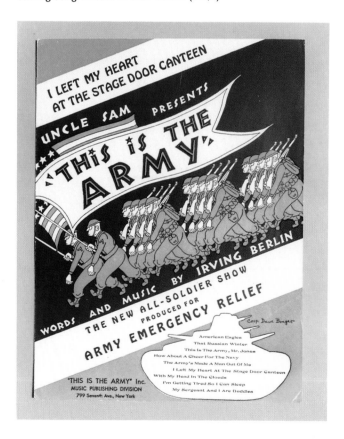

I Left My Heart at the Stage Door Canteen
Song from Irving Berlin' wartime musical *This Is the Army* was sung by a soldier who falls in love with a girl named Eileen at the Stage Door Canteen. (1942)

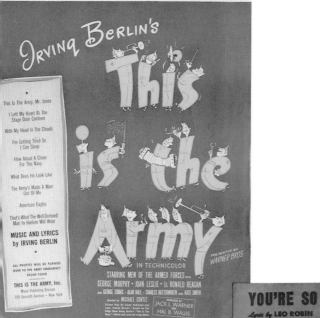

This Is The Army, Mr. Jones

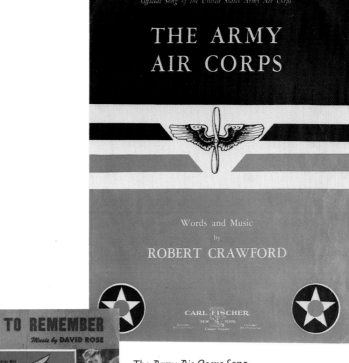

This Is the Army, Mister Jones
The sergeant looked over a bunch of frightened rookies, then laid down the law "…no private rooms or telephones… we like the barracks nice and clean." (1942)

You're So Sweet to Remember
20th Century-Fox in association with the U. S. Army Air Forces produced a movie adaptation of *Winged Victory* in 1944 featuring this nostalgic song.

The Army Air Corps Song
Official U. S. Army Air Corps song written by Robert M. Crawford in 1939 was played throughout the play *Winged Victory*.

Any Bonds Today?
Irving Berlin's rousing song persuaded Americans everywhere to buy bonds and stamps to help win the war for freedom. (1941)

Winged Victory
Sergeant David Rose wrote the title song for the Army Air Forces show benefiting the U.S. Army Emergency Relief Fund. (1943)

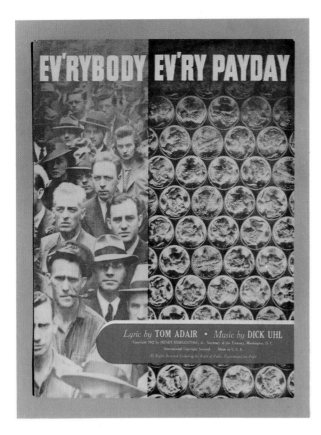

Ev'rybody Ev'ry Payday
Liberty head dimes adorn sheet music cover of song that urges everybody to take a dime from every dollar and buy bonds for Uncle Sam. (1942)

There's a New Flag on Iwo Jima
The raising of the U. S. flag on the hill Suribachi inspired this tribute to the Marines written by Harold Adamson to music by Jimmy McHugh. (1945)

"Buy a Bond Today" was another effective promotional piece. The famous photograph of the raising of the American flag atop Mount Suribachi by five Marines and a Navy corpsman taken by Associated Press photographer Joe Rosenthal is reproduced on the cover. The U.S. Marines had landed on Iwo Jima on February 10, 1945, and suffered heavy losses in the capture of this important air base. In 34 days of fighting there were 20,196 casualties, of which 4,305 were killed. The battle is further commemorated in the songs "Stars and Stripes on Iwo Jima" and "There's a New Flag on Iwo Jima."

Pride in serving one's country was manifested in songs written in praise of different branches of the military machine. "The Song of the Seabees" was printed for complimentary distribution by the Bureau of Yards and Docks of the United States Navy. It is dedicated to the SEABEES Construction and Fighting Men of the United States Navy. The back cover is a recruitment promotional to "Join the Navy SEABEES," with a full description of duties and benefits, and where to apply. Other branches of the service similarly showed emblems on covers of songs espousing loyalty and pride.

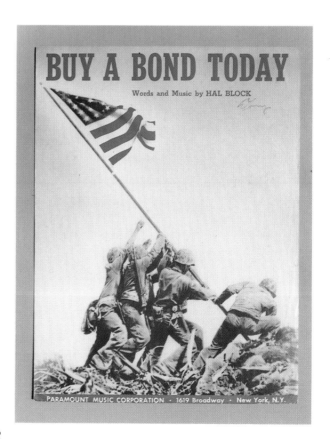

Buy a Bond Today
Famous picture on cover of this patriotic song by Hal Block helped to sell war bonds. (1944)

Guadalcanal March
Musical interpretation of a World War II battle was composed by
Richard Rodgers for his epic *Victory at Sea*. (1952)

The Song of the Seabees
Complimentary promotional song by the United States Navy extols
the bravery and dedication of the Construction Regiment's
"SEABEES." (1942)

Song of the Signal Corps
Dedicated to the United States Signal Corps, this song has stirring
lyrics, "...we'll pack walkie-talkies and set up poles, splice up our
cables shot full of holes ...for the sun can't set on our short wave
net..." (1943)

The Men of the Yorktown March
John Williams' march was played in the movie *Midway*, a
dramatization of the air-sea battle fought in the Pacific off Midway
Island in which the aircraft carrier *Yorktown* was sunk by the
Japanese. (1976)

133

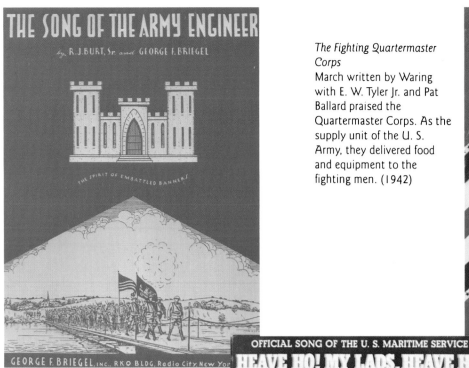

The Fighting Quartermaster Corps
March written by Waring with E. W. Tyler Jr. and Pat Ballard praised the Quartermaster Corps. As the supply unit of the U. S. Army, they delivered food and equipment to the fighting men. (1942)

The Song of the Army Engineer
The army engineers embody the "Spirit of Embattled Banners." "…The Captain says my rifle's rusty…if he'd inspect my pick and shovel, he'd find them shining bright." (1939)

Heave Ho! My Lads, Heave Ho!
Lieutenant (j.g.) Jack Lawrence U.S.M.S. wrote this official song of the U. S. Maritime Service at the training station at Sheepshead Bay, Brooklyn, New York. (1943)

The Men of the Merchant Marine
Jack Dolph and Fred Waring wrote about the unsung heroes of the Merchant Marine who aided the war effort by transporting bombs, bullets, fuel, and troops overseas. "I've carried guns to Singapore, munitions to Ceylon, I carried wheat for the boys to eat with MacArthur at Bataan… I've seen my share of submarines, and heard torpedoes blaze, I've been afloat in an open boat over thirty thirsty days…" (1942)

Sky Anchors
Fred Waring was commissioned to write this official Naval Aviation song by the Officers and Cadets of the U. S. Naval Air Station at Pensacola, Florida. Cover shows Douglas SBD Dauntless dive bombers that fought at the battle of Midway. (1942)

The Navy Hymn
Staunch Naval officer stands watch on the cover of the official Navy hymn with words by W. Whiting and music by J. B. Dykes. (1943)

Roll Tanks Roll
The men of the armored forces were honored in this song by Fred Waring and Jack Dolph with words, "Roll, tanks, roll...leap, jeep, leap." (1942)

Anchors Aweigh
President Franklin D. Roosevelt had a special affection for the Navy, and was Assistant Secretary of the Navy during the Wilson administration from 1913-1921. (1935 reprint)

Semper Paratus
Official Coast Guard marching song shows a Coast Guard cutter, a lifeboat from Station No. 23 propelled by oars, and Coast Guard seaplane No. 132 surrounding the official seal. Song was composed by Van Boskerck in 1928. (1942 reprint)

The Marines' Hymn
Special 1942 edition of the Marine Corps' official song promoted the 20th Century-Fox movie *To the Shores of Tripoli* starring, left to right, Randolph Scott, Maureen O'Hara, and John Payne. Song was written in 1917 by Sergeant L. Z. Phillips.

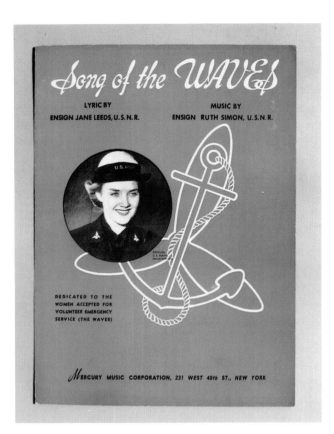

Song of the WAVES
This well-written song by two women in the United States Naval Reserve, Ensigns Jane Leeds and Ruth Simon, was dedicated to the Women Accepted for Volunteer Emergency Service, "The WAVES." (1943)

March of the Women Marines
Official march of the Marine Corps Women's Reserve was written by members of the U.S. Marine Band, Emil Grasser and Louis Saverino. "…We serve that men may fight in air, on land, and sea." (1943)

The Caissons Go Rolling Along
Featured in the 20th Century-Fox movie *Ten Gentlemen from West Point*, this 1921 march by Brigadier General Edmund L. Gruber was dedicated to the U. S. Field Artillery. Cover stars, left to right, George Montgomery, Maureen O'Hara, and John Sutton. (1945)

The Bombardier Song
Cover photo shows bombardier gazing aloft at a World War II B-17 bomber. Dedicated to the Bomber Crews of the U.S. Army Air Forces by songwriters Rodgers and Hart who generously donated all profits to the Army Air Forces Aid Society Trust Fund. (1942)

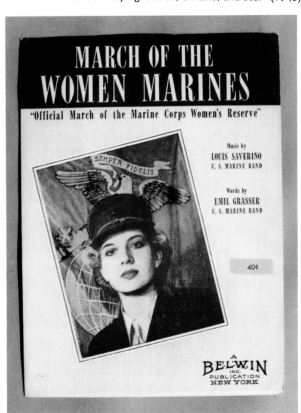

Before entering the service, talented Frank Loesser was the successful lyricist for such Hit Parade songs as "Jingle, Jangle, Jingle," "I Don't Want to Walk Without You," "Two Sleepy People," and "Small Fry." As a private in the Army he wrote both words and music about the agonies of basic training in the song, "What Do You Do In the Infantry" which was later designated the official marching song of the 264th Infantry Regiment of the 66th Black Panther Division.

Loesser was kept busy in the Army turning out requests from the various military branches for songs "First Class Private Mary Brown," "It's Great To Be in the Air Corps," "On the Beam," "The Sad Bombardier," "The WAC Hymn," "Why Do They Call a Private a Private?," and "The Road to Victory" for the Treasury Department which was used in connection with the Third War Loan Drive. He had the special ability to write songs that interpreted a GI's thoughts and yearnings. He will be long remembered for his morale building musical contributions to both GIs and civilians during World War II.

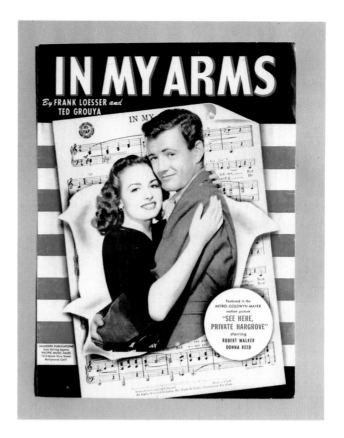

In My Arms
Song reflecting a soldier's longing to have a girl in his arms was used in the Metro-Goldwyn-Mayer movie *See Here, Private Hargrove* with stars Robert Walker and Donna Reed. Another edition has no pictorial cover, but begins the music on the front cover purportedly to save paper. (1943)

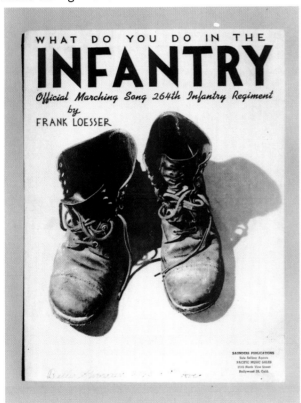

What Do You Do In the Infantry?
Composer Frank Loesser knew from personal experience the hardships and aching feet of the marching men of the infantry. (1943)

They're Either Too Young or Too Old
Loesser focused on the girls left behind in this humorous song performed by Bette Davis in the Warner Brothers all-star movie *Thank Your Lucky Stars.* Most of the studio's major stars are shown on the cover. (1943)

Loesser's most famous war song was "Praise the Lord and Pass the Ammunition" which was based on an actual heroic war episode. The story is told on the inside cover of the sheet music. The time was December 7th, 1941, during the Japanese attack on Pearl Harbor.

"...As sailors boiled from below decks of a U.S. Navy warship to fight off low flying Japanese planes, Chaplain William Maguire left his altar and ran to a gun station where one of the gunners had been killed and another wounded. In the unholy roar of that torrent of bombs, Chaplain Maguire shouted his now famous words: 'I just got one of them!! Praise the Lord and Pass the Ammunition!!'"

Praise The Lord And Pass The Ammunition!!

Praise the Lord and Pass the Ammunition!! Frank Loesser was inspired by these exciting words to fashion his stirring battle song. As a further gesture of patriotism he donated all his royalties from the sale of the song to the Navy Relief Society. (1942)

Rodger Young Rodger Young was a GI folk hero, a Congressional Medal of Honor winner from Ohio who had been killed in the Solomons. Loesser dedicated this ballad "To those heroic Infantrymen who, like Rodger Young, have sacrificed their lives that their Nation might remain forever free." (1945)

Dwight David Eisenhower was one of the most popular American heroes of his time, an effective U.S. general and tactician and a distinguished statesman and President. As a graduate of the U.S. Military Academy at West Point in 1915 he requested overseas combat duty during World War I, but was instead assigned duty at training camps because of his outstanding leadership skills. These abilities won for him the coveted position of supreme commander of Western Allied forces during World War II where he commanded the invasion of North Africa in November 1942 and the Normandy Invasion on D-Day June 6 1944. He was elected 34th President of the United States in 1952 and served two terms.

General George Patton was another graduate of West Point, and saw tank service in France in World War I. He was a tough indomitable field commander during World War II earning the nickname "Old Blood and Guts." He was a tough disciplinarian and received much unfavorable publicity for slapping a shell-shocked soldier in a hospital, and calling him a yellow coward.

His achievements were many. He commanded ground forces in the invasion of North Africa in 1942, and aided in the capture of Sicily in 1943. Following the Allies' Normandy invasion, he drove his Third Army across France into Germany in 1944-45. An able tank commander, he halted the German counterattack in the Battle of the Bulge, and relieved the 101st Airborne Division at Bastogne.

A March to Eisenhower
This tribute to Eisenhower was issued as a souvenir on the occasion of his inauguration as 34th President of the United States. (1953)

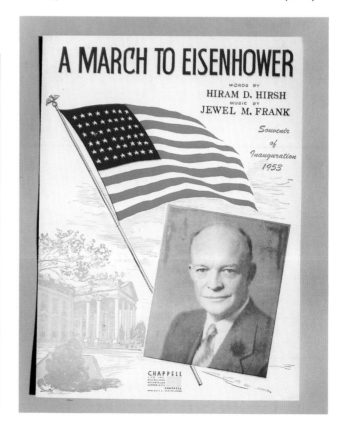

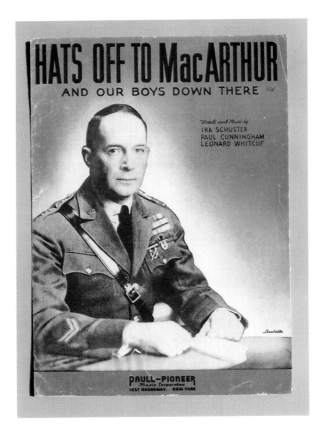

Patton Theme
George C. Scott's magnificent portrayal of the crusty general in the 20th Century-Fox movie *Patton* earned for both him and the film an Academy Award. (1970)

Hats Off to MacArthur
This stirring tribute to the popular General has a cover photo showing him in uniform without his omnipresent hat. (1942)

General Douglas MacArthur was a distinguished hero of World War II who was honored in popular song. As a young man he had graduated first in his class from the U. S. Military academy, fought and was wounded during World War I, and served his country brilliantly through many long years. He ultimately became a five star general, and the commander of U. S. Army forces in the Pacific. A divergence of political views led to his dismissal by President Truman in 1951.

MacArthur's moving speech to Congress on April 19, 1951, is commemorated in the song "Old Soldiers Never Die" by Lt. Barry Drewes, with an excerpt from the speech on the back cover.

"I am closing my fifty-two years of military service.... I still remember the refrain of one of the most popular barrack ballads which proclaimed most proudly that old soldiers never die; they just fade away. And like the old soldier of that ballad, I now close my military career and just fade away, an old soldier who tried to do his duty as God gave him the light to see that duty. Good by."

Old Soldiers Never Die (They Just Fade Away)
Touching ballad lauds the old patriot, "Fare thee well, old soldier, though you're gone, your deeds live on." This version is based on the 1939 song by Frank Westphal. (1951)

Our Miracle Man
Song dedicated to MacArthur calls him a miracle man, a fearless leader who will lead us on to victory, "...he charts the way our airmen go, they carry bombs marked Tokio." (1942)

Lili Marleen
German edition of the hit song with words by Hans Leip has cover photo of singer Lale Andersen who introduced it. (1940)

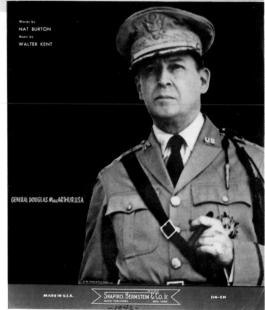

Here's to You, MacArthur
March song by Nat Burton and Walter Kent praises MacArthur as "the soldier in the Pacific whom the Japs don't like at all." (1942)

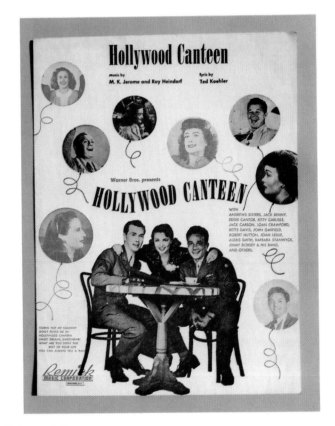

Hollywood Canteen
During the war, Hollywood movie stars donated their time and talent to the Hollywood Canteen, where a serviceman could dance with his favorite pinup girl. Song was featured in the Warner Brothers all-star movie *Hollywood Canteen*. (1944)

A prominent composer and Nazi propagandist, Norbert Schultze, composed a World War II song that was embraced by not only the Germans but also the Allied soldiers. "Lili Marleen" was sung by Lale Andersen, a popular German cabaret singer, over a German short-wave radio station in Belgrade to Rommel's troops in North Africa in 1941. The program was picked up by both German and British troops in Africa, and soon became an international hit. An American version with words by Mack David and music by Phil Park was introduced in the United States by chanteuse Hildegard in 1943.

World War II produced its share of movie songs. The star-studded movie *Hollywood Canteen*, about two soldiers on sick leave in Hollywood, saluted the war effort of Hollywood stars who served coffee and sandwiches and entertainment to lonely young servicemen at the famous Hollywood Canteen.

The Canteen Bounce
The canteen was the place to eat, dance, and play for the serviceman. Jazzy song tells of a contemporary dance called the canteen bounce that has the dancers "jumpin' like a jumpin' bean." Cover photo of orchestra leader Charlie Spivak. (1943)

As Time Goes By
Dooley Wilson as Sam sang this romantic 1931 song for Humphrey Bogart and Ingrid Bergman at Rick's Cafe in the popular Warner Brothers wartime drama *Casablanca*. Also on cover is second lead Paul Henreid. (1943)

How Blue the Night
Featured song in the 20th Century-Fox movie *Four Jills in a Jeep*, the story of the real-life exploits of four actresses (Carole Landis, Martha Raye, Mitzi Mayfair, and Kay Francis) who entertained the troops in Europe during WW II. Also seen on cover are singer Dick Haymes and Jimmy Dorsey playing the sax. (1944)

Other memorable ballads were used in wartime movies, often as theme songs. Who can forget the nostalgic "As Time Goes By" which will forever be associated with Humphrey Bogart and Ingrid Bergman in the movie classic *Casablanca?*" The movie was filmed in 1942 before the historic meeting at Casablanca of Roosevelt and Churchill with the Free French General Charles de Gaulle and General Henri Giraud, High Commissioner of French Africa.

Linda
Song is from the gripping movie *Story of G. I. Joe*, with story line based on the observations of respected war correspondent Ernie Pyle who wrote about the misery of the infantryman during the bloody Italian campaign. (1945)

I Came Here to Talk
For Joe
The close harmony
of the Four King
Sisters enhanced
this poignant song
that tells of a
message from Joe
to his girlfriend.
(1942)

Sweetheart of All My Dreams
Thirty Seconds Over Tokyo, an important wartime movie about the
Doolittle raid over Tokyo, starred Spencer Tracy as Doolittle and Van
Johnson as the pilot, Captain Ted Lawson. The movie received critical
accolades for the integrity of its wartime scenes. (1945)

*I Don't Want to
Walk Without You*
Song from the
movie *Sweater Girl*
became a huge
success when
taken up by
recording star
Helen Forrest,
singing with Harry
James and his
orchestra. (1941)

Popular Wartime Ballads

I'll Be Seeing You
"...in all the old
familiar places
...that small cafe
...the park across
the way, the
children's carousel,
the chestnut trees,
the wishing well."
Though written in
1938, this song
didn't become a hit
until after the war
started and the
words took on new
meaning.
Bandleader Freddy
Martin on cover.
(1943)

No Love, No Nothin'
As introduced by Alice Faye in the 20th Century-Fox movie, *The
Gang's All Here*, this became a popular wartime torch song. (1943)

I'll Be With You in Apple Blossom Time
Sentimental 1920 ballad was revived in the movie *Buck Privates* becoming an enormous hit as sung by the harmony trio The Andrews Sisters. (1941)

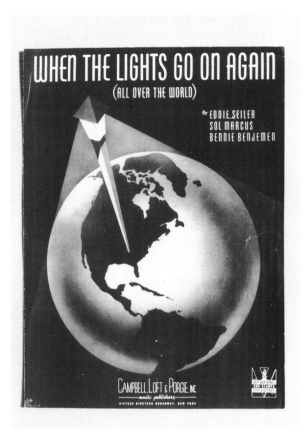

When the Lights Go On Again (All Over the World)
Song sounds a note of optimism about the sweet and simple life when the war is over. (1942)

Savin' Myself for Bill
Sergeant Ginny Simms, the silken-voiced singer, presented this wartime song on NBC's radio show *Johnny Presents*. (1942)

The Shrine of St. Cecilia
Though the town was in a shambles after destruction rained from the skies, the shrine up on the hillside was spared, and remained a place of comfort and solace. (1941)

143

I Had a Little Talk With the Lord
This song was the prayer of a battle-weary boy in a foxhole in Bougainville asking for faith and strength to continue to fight. (1944)

Comin' In on a Wing and a Prayer
The plane hit its target but lost an engine and limped home on a wing and a prayer in this Harold Adamson and Jimmy McHugh song popularized by Dick Haymes. (1943)

When I Heard Taps Blow that Night
Touching song by Sergeant Rahland Wilson is dedicated to his friend Corporal Jimmy Schnell of the Second Marine Parachute Battalion. (1944)

The House I Live In
Frank Sinatra sang this patriotic emotional song in an RKO featurette, considered by many one of the finest songs to come out of World War II. (1942)

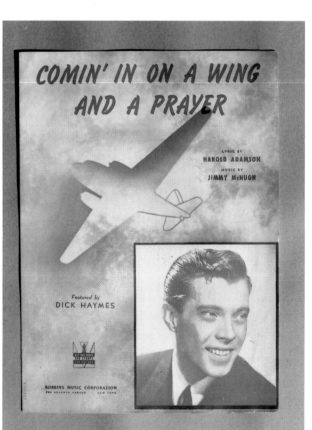

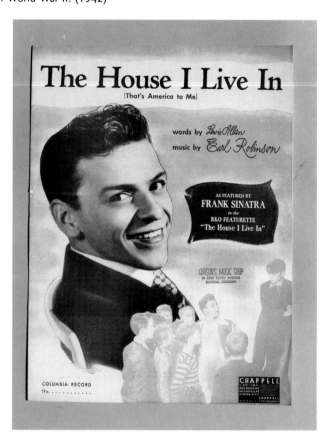

"There Goes My Sailor Boy," written by Ethel Verity Hofstra, shows a mother's pride in her son and the U. S. Navy. Above the lyrics on the back cover she wrote, "I dedicate this song to give courage to other mothers with boys in the U. S. Navy in loving memory of George and the USS *Lexington*." The aircraft carrier *Lexington* was sunk in the Coral Sea in May of 1942.

Mail Call and Memories

Letters from the front were anxiously awaited at home, and songs about servicemen taking pen in hand appeared. Memories of home, sweetheart, and family were frequent themes of popular wartime songs, as well as the plight of the lonely serviceman.

There Goes My Sailor Boy
Courageous Ethel Verity Hofstra honored her son with this song she wrote in his memory. George Hofstra is on cover, second from the left, with his initials circled. (1942)

At Mail Call Today
Cowboy star Gene Autry who served as flight officer with the Air Transport Command during World War II wrote this sad song about a soldier who received a "Dear John" letter from his faithless sweetheart. (1945)

Here Comes the Navy
Lieutenant Commander Clarence P. Oakes U.S.N.R. wrote the words to the melody of "Beer Barrel Polka" and donated his royalties from the sale to Navy Relief. (1943)

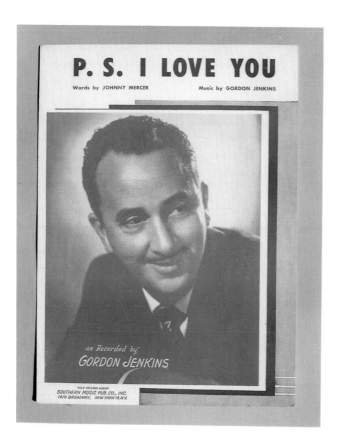

P.S. I Love You
Johnny Mercer wrote these poignant lyrics about a letter filled with
the mundane trivia of everyday life, leaving the most important part
of the message for the postscript. (1953 reprint of 1934 song)

White Christmas
One of Irving Berlin's most enduring songs had its start in the
entertaining Paramount movie *Holiday Inn* introduced by Bing
Crosby. (1942)

Wish You Were Here
Song was featured in the Universal comedy *Buck Privates* with cover
stars Bud Abbott and Lou Costello and the Andrews Sisters. (1941)

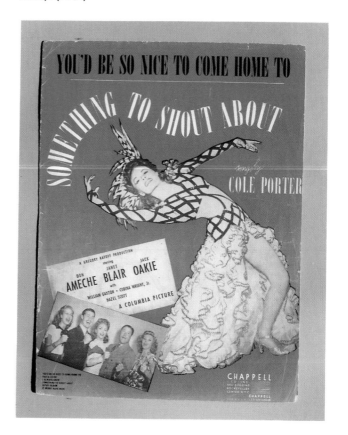

You'd Be So Nice to Come Home To
Cover stars Don Ameche and Janet Blair featured this lovely Cole
Porter song in Columbia Picture's *Something to Shout About.* (1942)

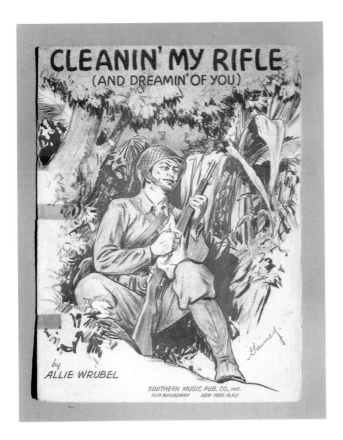

Cleanin' My Rifle (and Dreamin' of You)
During a lull in the battle a young soldier sitting around the camp waxes nostalgic as he dreams of the good days while cleaning his weapon. (1943)

Hot Time in the Town of Berlin (There'll Be a)
Sergeant Joe Bushkin and Private John De Vries wrote this aggressive song about the victorious Yanks marching into Berlin. (1943)

Spirited Fighting Songs

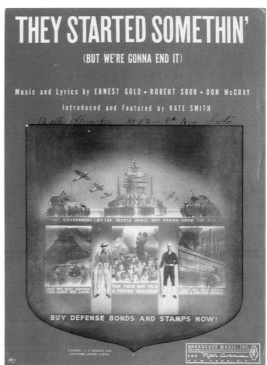

They Started Somethin'
Patriotic upbeat march song promoting war bond sales was introduced by Kate Smith in 1942.

Johnny Zero
Clever lyrics by Mack David tells of Johnny who got zero grades in school growing up to become an ace pilot getting Zeros in the air. (1943)

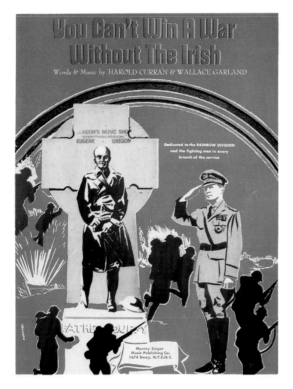

You Can't Win a War Without the Irish
Dedicated to the Rainbow Division. Cover drawing shows heroes Father Duffy and General MacArthur; lyrics salute the Fighting Sixty-Nines and a million other Irish Yanks. (1942)

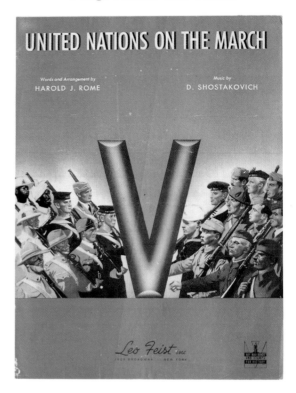

United Nations on the March
Russian composer Dimitri Shostakovich wrote this tribute to the United Nations with words by Harold J. Rome. (1942)

The Fuehrer's Swan-Song
Song mocks Hitler, "…He conquered countries one by one until the Red Bear stopped his blitz! He'll freeze there like Napoleon, if he doesn't call it quits!" R. Fabri's imaginative cover shows Hitler singing his farewell swan-song. (1943)

You Can't Win this War Through Love! Song urges country to be tough. "…in fighting wars you can't be nice… know your enemies, they are rough!" Garish cover by R. Fabri. (1943)

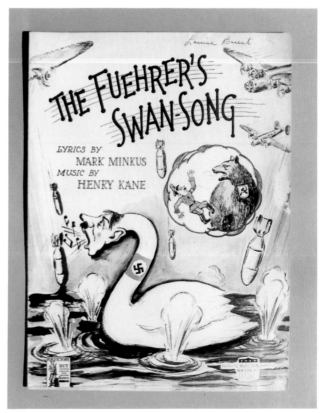

Hitler invaded the USSR on June 22, 1941, in a campaign called Operation Barbarossa. Despite initial successes in Russia, the Germans eventually succumbed to the inclement weather, severe snowstorms and subzero temperatures, and lack of supplies that left them weak and vulnerable to a counterattack by the indomitable "Russian Bear." In February 1943 after the bloody Battle of Stalingrad where the Germans were defeated, the tides of war began to turn in the Allies' favor.

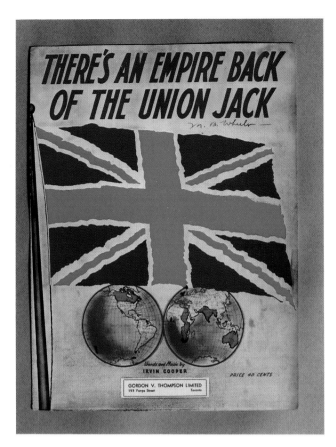

There's an Empire Back of the Union Jack
This song published in Canada promises, "…We'll never fail Old England…Stout hearts from the Empire bringing help for the motherland." (1941)

Meadowlands
An army of Russian foot soldiers armed with rifles and bayonets march purposefully across the Steppes on cover of powerful song translated from the Russian. (1944)

And Russia Is Her Name
Russia is romanticized in this song by Jerome Kern and E. Y. Harburg from the Metro-Goldwyn-Mayer movie *Song of Russia* starring Robert Taylor and Susan Peters. (1943)

Wartime Songs in a Lighter Vein

Rum and Coca-Cola
"…both mother and daughter working' for the Yankee dollar…" Slightly bawdy lyrics and a lilting Calypso rhythm added to the charm of this hit song of the Andrews Sisters. (1944)

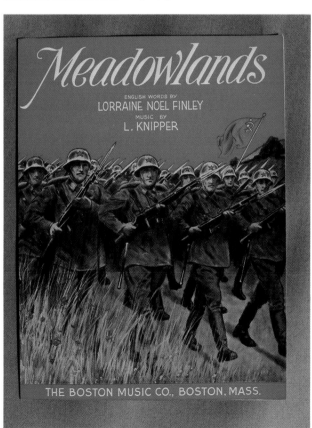

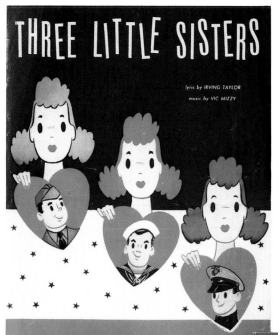

Bell Bottom Trousers
Innocent words and music by Moe Jaffe were soon augmented by shady verses that no lady should hear! The simple stanzaic form of the song was a "natural" for improvised verses. (1944)

Three Little Sisters
"One loved a soldier, one loved a sailor, and one loved a lad from the Marines." The three little sisters promised to be true until the boys came home. (1942)

Sound Off
Considered by many to be the greatest thing in the world to make a thousand men march together without stepping on each other, this U.S. Army cadence chant was written by Willie Lee Duckworth. The men would extemporize as they marched, and many verses were passed by word of mouth. (1950)

G.I. Jive
Johnny Mercer wrote this humorous tribute to the American soldier about the rigors of life in the army. The cover tells it all—a hapless private dancing with a picture of his girl instead of peeling the pile of potatoes at his feet, and a glowering top sergeant ready to "chew him out." (1943)

Don't Sit Under the Apple Tree
This musical admonition by a soldier to his girl was a popular wartime hit. Glenn Miller made a lively recording with Tex Beneke, Marion Hutton, and the Modernaires. (1942)

Move It Over
Sunny Skylar's bouncy song tells of a burly sergeant ordering a private to move endless piles of dirt. (1942)

Der Fuehrer's Face
This broad parody of Nazism mocked both Hitler and Goebbels, and referred in broken German lyrics to "nutzis" instead of Nazis. It was written for the Disney cartoon *Donald Duck in Nutzi Land*. (1942)

If the Boys Come Home for Christmas
1943 song anticipated the happy day when servicemen would be home for Christmas, but it wasn't until August of 1945 that peace came at last.

I'm Gonna Love That Guy (Like He's Never Been Loved Before)
Returning servicemen were ecstatic to be greeted with sentiments like this written by Frances Ash and performed by Kay Armen. (1945)

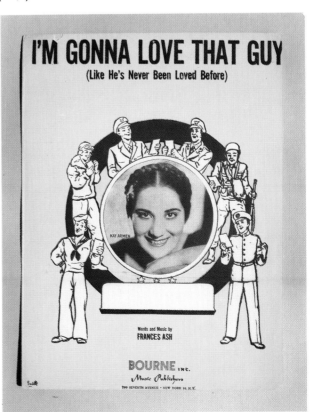

Roaring Volcano
E. T. Paull explains his musical conception of this march as imitative
of violent volcanic bursts. Chromolithograph cover shows the huge
volcano spewing rocks, fire, and molten lava on to the town below.
(1912)

CHAPTER 4: NOTEWORTHY NEWS

Seldom did an event of any importance go unnoticed by Tin Pan Alley songwriters. Music was written for almost every occasion, pieces that are representative of the history and changing times in America. Political events, elections, legislation, natural disasters, murders, kidnapping, trials, discoveries, and dedications are some of the occasions commemorated in popular sheet music.

1. Disasters

Attention-getting news stories of the day dealt with disasters and misfortunes. Great natural disasters of yore—floods, earthquakes, and fires—were written about in song. The great volcanic eruption of Mount Vesuvius buried the nearby city of Pompeii in A.D. 79, and two marches with fantastic covers were written in commemoration.

Another ancient disaster of colossal proportions was memorialized in music by E. T. Paull. He wrote "The Burning of Rome" about the dreadful fire in A.D. 64 that destroyed most of the city. The cover lithography by A. Hoen & Company produced a brilliant illustration of the conflagration, showing the blazing city reflected in the Tiber River with Nero safely fiddling on the opposite shore. Not only is Paull's music especially evocative and suitable to the subject, but the cover illustrations are without doubt among the finest examples of sheet music lithography. Two other disastrous events have very fine action covers by the Paull company.

The Burning of Rome
E. T. Paull typically used representational musical effects simulating alarms, panic-stricken people rushing wildly though the streets, fiercely raging fires, and walls crashing down. (1903)

Last Days of Pompeii
March and two-step by Caird M. Vandersloot has a dramatic cover of the cataclysmic eruption drawn by Dittmar. (1904)

Ships going down at sea were dramatic events that stunned the nation, and inspired an outpouring of memorial songs. Probably the most famous maritime disaster was the sinking of the *Titanic* in 1912. The *Titanic* was a White Star passenger liner, the largest ship afloat at that time. On her maiden voyage from Southampton to New York she struck an iceberg in the North Atlantic. Lifeboat accommodations were inadequate, and a reported 1503 persons were lost at sea. Several songs were written in 1912 about the disaster.

The Hurricane
This march was composed by S. L. Alpert and arranged by E. T. Paull. The lithography is by A. Hoen and Company of Richmond, Virginia. (1906)

The Midnight Fire Alarm
Harry J. Lincoln wrote this piece with special arrangement by E. T. Paull. Lithograph by A. Hoen Company shows a fine example of early firefighting apparatus. (1907)

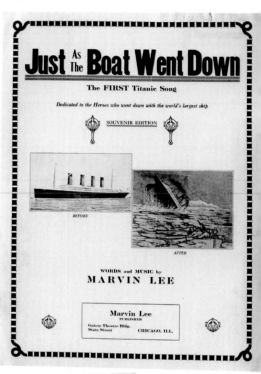

Just As the Boat Went Down
This souvenir edition is dedicated to the heroes who went down with the world's largest ship. Notable are the before and after pictures—a photo of the *Titanic* in pristine glory, and a drawing as she sinks into the sea. (1912)

Just As the Ship Went Down
Edith Maida Lessing wrote the dramatic words with music by Bernie Adler and Sidney Gibson. The cover illustration (courtesy of the *Chicago Record-Herald*) shows people in lifeboats gazing in shocked horror as the great ship lists perilously in the sea with an enormous iceberg looming ominously in the background. (1912)

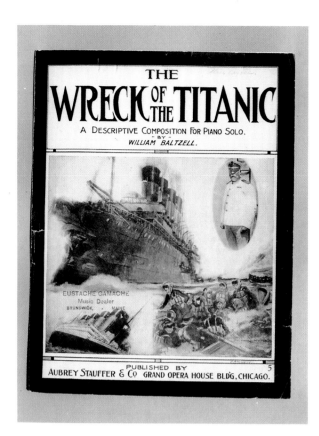

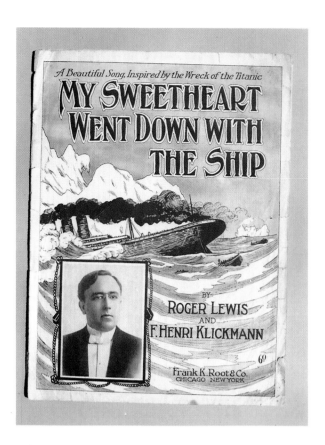

The Wreck of the Titanic (by Baltzell)
The music represents events that happened at sea, complete with explanatory captions. Cover design by Z. A. Hendrick shows lifeboats being lowered into the sea from the capsizing ship, and a photo inset of Ship's Captain Edward J. Smith. A black funeral wreath on the back cover has the inscription "In Memoriam, to the brave musicians who played the last requiem for the passengers of the *Titanic*." (1912)

My Sweetheart Went Down with the Ship
Dreadful event is romanticized in popular song, telling of the hero who gave his life that women and children could be saved. (1912)

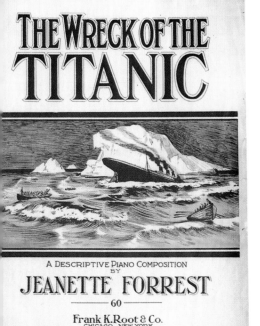

The Wreck of the Titanic (by Forrest)
Effectively ending this piece by Jeanette Forrest is the melody of "Nearer My God To Thee" intoned in the left hand bass part accompanied by broken chords in the right hand, with directions to grow fainter and fainter until the song ends—a dramatic finish. (1912)

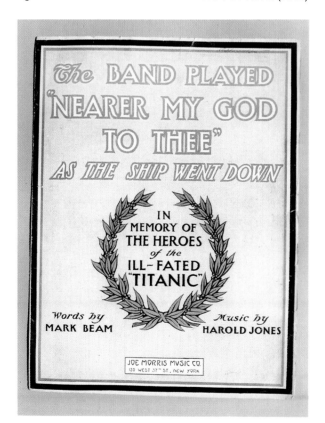

The Band Played "Nearer My God to Thee" As the Ship Went Down
The strains of the fine old hymn wafted across the sea as the ship plunged to her final rest. Written in memory of the heroes of the ill-fated *Titanic*. (1912)

The "Three Bells Polka" commemorates another disaster at sea. Legend on the front cover below the illustration contains the eulogy:

"The gallant conduct of Captain Creighton of the ship Three Bells *in risking his own life to save those of his fellow beings on board the ill fated* San Francisco *has won for him the admiration of the world and made him the object of innumerable honours and eulogies."*

Three Bells Polka
This instrumental piece was dedicated to Captain Creighton by T. J. Cook. Lithograph by Sarony, Major, & Knapp of New York. (1853)

Other songs about disasters at sea that the dogged collector may find are:

"Grace Darling or the Wrecker's Daughter" by George Lindley, dedicated to Grace Horsley Darling who, with her father, rescued nine persons from the wreck of the steamer *Forfarshire* (1850);

"The Lost Steamer" by Sarony about the wreck of the *Pacific*, a Collins Line steamer missing in the North Atlantic (1856);

"Lost on the *Lady Elgin*" by Henry C. Work about the terrible disaster on Lake Michigan on 7 September 1860 when the excursion steamer *Lady Elgin* collided with a lumber ship killing 300 (1861);

"I Do Not Want to Be Drowned" by Frank Soule Esq. and P. R. Nicholls, dedicated to the survivors of the wreck of the *Golden-Gate* which burned at sea (1862);

"Lost on the Steamer *Stonewall* or O Mamma! Why Don't Papa Come Home?" by J. S. Murphy and G. W. Brown, about the steamer *Stonewall* that burned on the Mississippi River below Cairo, Illinois, with a loss of 200 lives (1869);

"Kiss Me Mamma for I Am Going to Sleep" by J. A. Butterfield relates "A touching incident of two beautiful children who were on board the ill-fated steamship *Metis* wrecked on Long Island Sound Aug. 30, 1872;

"The Old *Kearsarge*" by W. O. Johnson was dedicated to the officers and sailors of the wrecked USS *Kearsarge* (1894);

"The Rescue of the *Antinoe*" by Al Sherman and Charles Tobias (1926).

On April 18, 1906, a great earthquake struck San Francisco tearing the beautiful city asunder. The devastation was completed by the wildfires which sprang up in a hundred different places, resulting from broken gas pipes, crossed electric wires, and the overturning of oil lamps. The quake also broke the water mains, and the fire department was helpless to fight the flames. For three days the fire devoured the city until it burned itself out. The total loss of lives in the catastrophe was listed at about 1,000, and total damages at about $350,000,000.

The song "San Francisco" by J. Gordon Temple and James G. Dewey is a fine historical piece that was released as a souvenir edition by the composer in New York. The cover design by Starmer has photographs of scenes around San Francisco before and after the quake. Three pictures before the earthquake and fire show the St. Francis Hotel and Dewey Monument in Union Square, the old Cliff House and Seal Rocks, and a view of the Golden Gate at sunset. The center picture shows San Francisco in flames. Another shot shows the ruins left by the fire with City Hall in the distance. The inside cover gives a graphic description of the San Francisco disaster.

Opposite Page, Center Left:
The Hum of the Hammer
The rebuilding of San Francisco started almost immediately. Valiant, irrepressible workers toiled day and night to restore the city to her former glory. "...Drive, boys, drive with all your might, It's up to you to rebuild our San Francisco." (1906)

Opposite Page. Bottom Left:
San Francisco
This collector's jewel commemorates the terrible San Francisco quake of 1906.

San Francisco
Metro-Goldwyn-Mayer movie recreated the dramatic earthquake, and starred Jeanette Macdonald and Clark Gable as fictional characters. (1936)

All through history, disastrous fires took their toll, and had songs written about them. In 1871 the Great Chicago Fire began in a barn and raged for two days. More than three miles in the heart of the city were burned over and 250 lives were lost. The following year another terrible fire destroyed the richest quarter of Boston with 65 acres burned over and 776 buildings destroyed leaving countless homeless people.

Six hundred and two people lost their lives in the Iroquois Theater fire in Chicago on December 30, 1903. The holocaust started during a holiday matinee of *Mr. Bluebeard* starring Eddie Foy. This fire led to more stringent safety regulations in theaters all over the world.

In Old Chicago
The conflagration in Chicago was simulated in the 20th Century-Fox movie *In Old Chicago* with cover stars from left to right, Tyrone Power, Alice Faye, and Don Ameche. (1937)

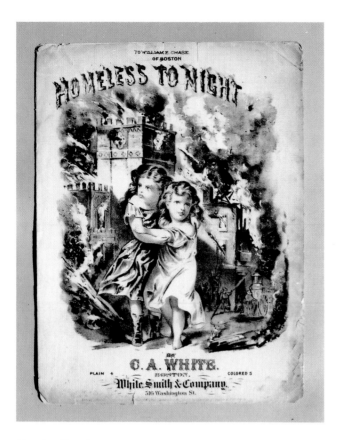

Homeless Tonight
Dramatic lithograph depicts two small frightened children escaping from a burning building during the Boston fire. For collectors interested in fire fighting apparatus, an old pumper also appears on the cover. (1874)

The Great Johnstown Flood of 1889 was an appalling disaster that took the lives of an estimated 2,200 people. The bursting of the South Fork Reservoir on the Conemaugh River let out millions of tons of water which descended on the borough of Johnstown at the mouth of Stony creek. A wall of water and debris twenty feet or more in height at its head almost completely destroyed Johnstown. A great mass of wreckage piled up against the Pennsylvania railroad bridge on which many people took refuge only to perish when the debris caught fire.

Winter storms in January and February 1937 buffeted the Ohio basin, and caused record-breaking flooding of the Ohio River. The disastrous flood crested at 80 feet in Cinncinnati, and inundated 12,700 square miles, affecting every major city on the Ohio and lower Mississippi rivers. 250 people died from drowning, and thousands more were left homeless when 75,000 homes were damaged or destroyed. Property damage exceeded $300,000,000. The song "Rising River" sounds like a spiritual—slow, solemn, minor, and dirge-like—a supplication imploring the river to rise no more.

The Torrents Came Upon Them, or the Johnstown Disaster
Tom Hall and George Schleiffarth wrote about the disastrous Johnstown flood. The cover lithograph illustrates the bridge with flaming wreckage behind it. (1889)

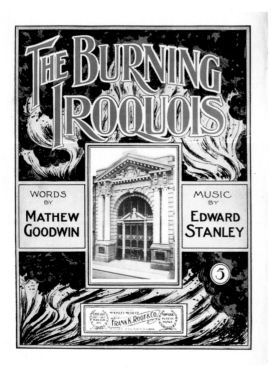

The Burning Iroquois
The magnificent Iroquois Theatre is shown on cover before the fire, and the dramatic ballad is bathed in pathos for the loss of so many loved ones. (1904)

Rising River
Profits from the sale of this song were donated by the publisher and composer to the relief of the 1937 flood victims. (1937)

2. Kidnapping, Murder, Evolution, and the Klan

Kidnapping always made big news. Sheet music was sometimes used to alert the public about the missing person with a photograph of the kidnap victim on the cover. Little nine-year-old Catherine Winters disappeared from the streets of New Castle, Indiana, at 11 a.m. on March 20, 1913, and was never seen again, and the sheet music pleaded for her return.

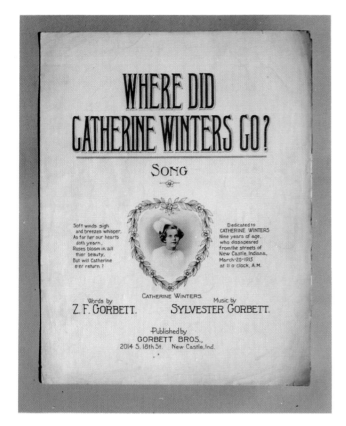

Where Did Catherine Winters Go?
"Have you seen the little darling who is missing from our town, or... Is her spirit with the angels and her form beneath the sod?" Lyrics ask for help in finding the child. (1914)

Even worse than the Catherine Winters case was the abduction of 12-year old Marion Parker on her way to school from her suburban home near Los Angeles on December 15, 1927. A ransom note was sent demanding $7,500 signed by "The Fox," followed by notes from little Marion herself. Her father eventually drove to an appointed rendezvous with the kidnapper and exchanged the money for a blanket-wrapped bundle left farther along the road. The anxious father unwrapped the bundle and found the grisly remains of his little daughter who had been strangled and dismembered. The vicious murderer was soon apprehended, twenty-three-year-old Edward Hickman, a college student who said he needed the money for tuition.

Despite his insanity plea, it didn't take a jury long to find him guilty of first degree murder, and he was hanged at San Quentin on October 19, 1928.

The eyes of the country were on the charismatic handsome couple Charles and Anne Morrow Lindbergh when they had a baby boy. Happy songs were written in the baby's honor, such as "Baby Lindy" by Clarence Gaskill and Irving Mills with its upbeat lyrics and its fetching cover of a baby in an airplane being towed by a stork.

In 1932 when the twenty month old Lindbergh infant was kidnaped and held for ransom, the outrage and compassion of the American people was expressed in songs "America's Duty to Lindbergh," "The Little Lost Eagle," and "Baby Lindy." The baby was eventually found dead, and Bruno Hauptmann was executed for the crime.

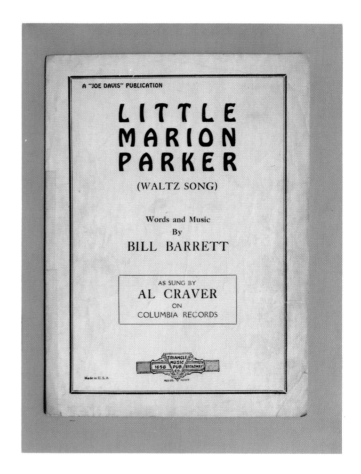

Little Marion Parker
The horrifying murder of 12-year-old Marion Parker inspired this song that warns parents, "We cannot guard too closely the ones we love so dear." (1928) *Collection of Carole Sealy*

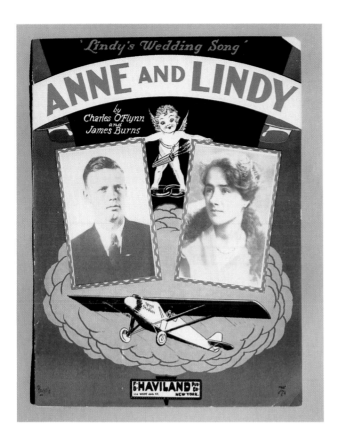

Anne and Lindy
America's romantic couple Anne Morrow and Charles Lindbergh are shown in happier times on the cover of "Lindy's Wedding Song" in 1929.

Find the Lindbergh Baby, Most Wanted in the Land
This stirring march incited the nation to search every building and woodland for the most wanted child in the land. (1932)

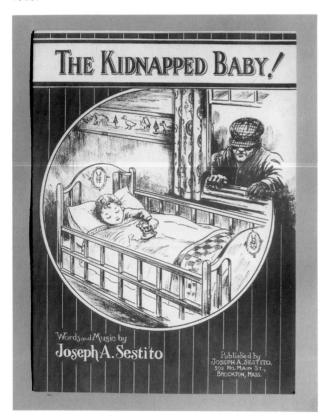

The Kidnapped Baby!
Shock and outrage were fomented with songs like this dramatic prayer for the safe return of the stolen baby to his heartbroken mother. (1932) *Collection of James Nelson Brown*

Crimes of passion also caught the eye of Tin Pan Alley songwriters. Scandal erupted in 1906 when Pittsburgh millionaire Harry Kendall Thaw murdered famous architect Stanford White, believing him to be having an affair with his wife, actress Evelyn Nesbit. Full details of the scandal were reported during the lurid trial, and a song sympathetic to Thaw and representative of his defense was written by Ross Edwards and Fred Leopold. Evelyn Nesbit had been a chorus girl before her marriage to the wealthy Thaw, and she continued her career after the trial, capitalizing on the attendant publicity.

The famous Scopes "monkey" trial came to public attention in 1925. John Thomas Scopes was tried for teaching evolution in public schools in violation of a Tennessee state law. The court debate centered on Charles Darwin's theory that man had evolved from apes, as set forth in his book *The Origin of the Species*. Two of the foremost legal minds of the time, William Jennings Bryan and Clarence Darrow debated science, religion, and the law for eleven days. Bryan, as the prosecutor, took a stand against evolution, quoting the Bible and relying more on fundamentalist beliefs than on scientific findings. Darrow took on the defense of Scopes without pay, and managed to discredit Bryan's case.

For the Sake of Wife and Home
Sympathies were slanted towards Harry Kendall Thaw who murdered his rival to protect his home. (1913)

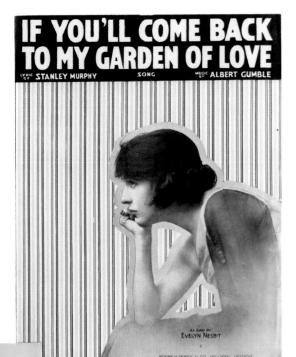

If You'll Come Back to My Garden of Love
Thaw's wife, beautiful singer/actress Evelyn Nesbit strikes a pensive pose on cover of song she performed. (1917)

There's Just a Little Bit of Monkey Still Left in You and Me
A song from Anna Held's show *Follow Me* refers to the Darwin theory and claims "…a girl made a monkey of me last night." (1916)

My Monkey Ma and Pa
This humorous ditty in Negro dialect pokes fun at the theory of evolution. The cover shows a father monkey pointing with pride to his son, a professor in cap and gown with a tome by Darwin under his arm. (1926)

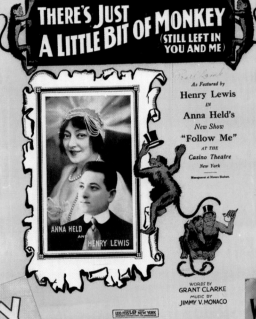

When My Great Grand Daddy and My Great Grand Mammy Used to Cuddly and Coo in a Cocoanut Tree
Songwriters Marshall Walker and Will Skidmore accept the theory of evolution and the notion that their forebears were chimpanzees in this funny syncopated song. (1917)

After the Civil War the country went through the throes of Reconstruction. In some states where Negroes were in the majority, whites were fearful that they would lose power in free elections, and resorted to terrorist tactics to keep Negroes from voting. Secret societies sprang up in many parts of the South—the most notorious being the Ku Klux Klan. The societies were effective though banned by Congress in 1871, and continued to function in secret with members in hooded apparel that disguised their identities.

Despite their questionable activities and radical ideas, the Klan was written about in song, with the songs frequently published by the writers themselves in what are known as vanity printings. The American flag, burning cross, and hooded rider on a rearing horse were frequent symbols on Klan song covers. Though one deplores the existence of the society, the songs are part of history and are collector's items.

Ku Klux Kismet
Cover shows typical Klansmen, hooded and gowned, one flourishing the American flag and the other brandishing a burning cross. (1924) *Collection of James Nelson Brown*

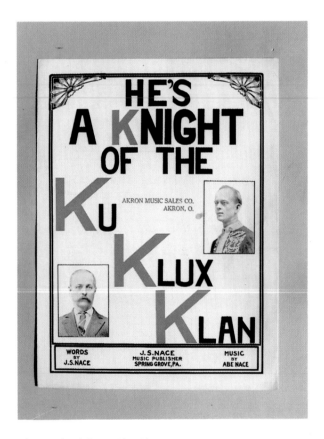

He's a Knight of the Ku Klux Klan
Jacob S. Nace and Abe Nace were proud of their Klan connections, and published their own Klan songs. Cover photos, though unidentified, are probably the Naces. (1924) *Collection of James Nelson Brown*

Mystic City
Cover shows glorification of knight on horseback with a glowing mystical city in the background, and lyrics, "Klansman of the Ku Klux Klan, Protestant, gentile, native born man...for their country's flag and heritage they die before they yield." (1922)

162

3. Prohibition

The country always had its share of alcohol related songs, from the early tearjerker "Come Home, Father" in 1864 to the good fellowship of the robust "Glorious Beer, Beer, Glorious Beer" in 1895. "Under the Anheuser Bush" lauds the wonders of beer as a young man and his girl at the beer garden lift their steins to "drink some Budwise under the Anheuser Bush."

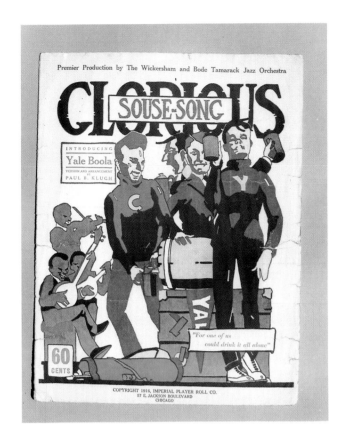

Glorious Souse Song
"Drunk last night, drunk the night before, goin' to get drunk tonight if I never get drunk anymore." 1916 fox trot introduces the "Yale Boola" song.

Under the Anheuser Bush
Harry Von Tilzer wrote the music and Andrew B. Sterling, the words, for this ode to the beer garden, "Picture Sue and me with our sandwich and stein." (1903)

For a while the moral do-gooders won out in the United States with the passage of the Volstead Act in 1919 over President Wilson's veto. It became the eighteenth amendment to the Constitution—the Prohibition amendment. From 1920 to 1933 the sale of beverages containing more than half of one per cent of alcohol was forbidden in the United States, and the song smiths went to work. Prohibition was to become effective January 16, 1920, but mild panic and dismay were already evident in the songs of 1919. "How Dry I Am" became the theme song of imbibers who still found their drinks, but in illegal ways. Speakeasies, bathtub gin, and bootlegging kept the alcohol flowing until the twenty-first amendment repealed federal Prohibition in 1933.

Down Where the Wurzburger Flows
Harry Von Tilzer teamed up with Vincent P. Bryan on this song, "…give me a piano, a cold stein of beer, and a fellow who knows how to play." (1902)

Prohibition Songs

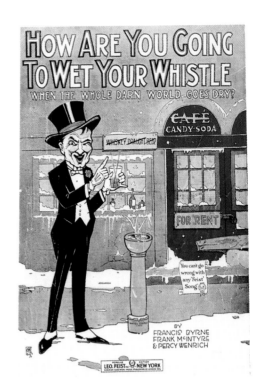

Whoa January (You're Going to Be Worse than July) Barbelle cover is a fine rendering of a distraught man in a blustery snowstorm peering at dusty bottles through the window of an empty saloon festooned with cobwebs. (1919)

How Are You Goin' to Wet Your Whistle? Rakish looking gentleman in evening clothes winks wickedly while brandishing a drink outside a padlocked cafe, and asks the question on everyone's lips in this Prohibition song by Percy Wenrich. (1919)

It's the Smart Little Feller Who Stocked Up His Cellar
The man with a cellar well stocked with booze has all the girls he wants in this Prohibition song. (1920)

I'll See You in C-U-B-A
Irving Berlin wrote this Prohibition song about one of the popular places to go after the U.S.A. "went dry." The lyrics suggested that drinking in a cellar isn't nice, and that it's better to go to Cuba where the wine is flowing freely. (1920)

I Married the Bootlegger's Daughter
Man found a way to survive Prohibition; he married the bootlegger's daughter, and is afloat in gin. Composer Frank Crumit on cover. (1925)

The Moon Shines on the Moonshine
Bert Williams' endearing shuffling character delighted audiences with this Prohibition song in Ziegfeld's *Follies*. The chorus, "How sad and still tonight, by the old distillery!" (1920)

Show Me the Way to Go Home
Favorite harmonizing song by Irving King has become an all-time favorite. This edition has nine extra verses. (1925)

Bartender Bill
Man waxes nostalgic outside a big drug store on the corner where Bartender Bill once poured drinks in a happy meeting place. (1930)

Just a Little Drink
Simple little song by Byron Gay asks for nothing else but a little drink. (1925)

4. The Great Depression

Beginning with the stock market crash of 1929, an economic crisis created havoc in the United States and other countries, continuing into the thirties. This period became known as the Great Depression. Unemployment, hunger, and despondency took over the country, and the outlook was bleak.

During the 1932 presidential campaign, Franklin Roosevelt coined the term "forgotten man," striking a responsive chord in the hundreds of men, many of whom had fought in the Great War, who were out of work. "Remember My Forgotten Man" by Al Dubin and Harry Warren was an effective Busby Berkeley production number in the *Gold Diggers of 1933*, a Depression movie musical that highlighted many of the social problems of the times.

"Underneath the Arches" by Bud Flanagan was a big hit in Europe before Bing Crosby featured it in the United States. The 1932 reprint by Robbins Music Corporation in New York has additional poignant lyrics by Joseph McCarthy about the plight of the homeless who sleep on cobblestones underneath a railroad bridge.

Underneath the Arches
Bing Crosby's eloquent rendition of this song engendered sympathy for the homeless with lyrics "...the pavement is my pillow no matter where I stray." (1932)

Remember My Forgotten Man
Cover star Joan Blondell performed this song in a lengthy production number featured in the Warner Brothers movie *Gold Diggers of 1933*.

Roosevelt's efforts to help the country get over the Depression in 1933 were centered on the National Recovery Act which used a small eagle and the letters NRA as its symbol. Employers who cooperated with the Act by establishing a five-day forty hour work week displayed the NRA eagle symbol with its slogan, "We Do Our Part." The little eagle symbol is seen on some of the sheet music from the early thirties indicating the cooperation of Tin Pan Alley.

Recovery was slow, but songs spawned by the Depression frequently effected a note of optimism about the hard times. Many of the popular titles philosophized about counting one's blessings; others reflected the despondency of the unemployed.

One of the brighter moments of the Depression was the birth of the Dionne quintuplets, born in Canada in 1934. The five darling babies only weighed collectively but 11-1/2 pounds six days after their premature birth, and were lavished with gifts and attention. To avoid exploitation they were made king's wards during their early childhood, but nonetheless, a stream of "quint" paper dolls, coloring books, and other souvenirs flooded the marketplace.

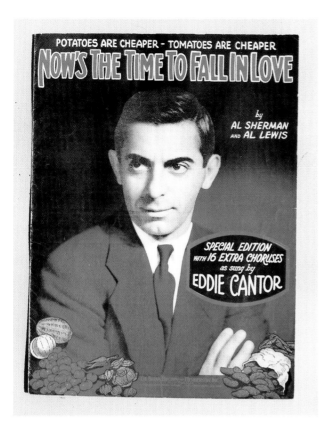

Now's the Time to Fall In Love
Eddie Cantor sang "Potatoes are cheaper, tomatoes are cheaper, two can live as cheap as one...now's the time to fall in love." (1931)

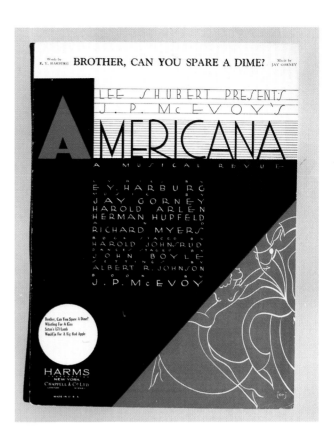

Brother, Can You Spare a Dime?
The depths of misery were plumbed in this Depression song, "...when there was earth to plough or guns to bear I was always there, ...why should I be standing in line just waiting for bread?" Song was popularized by Bing Crosby during those dark days. (1932)

Quintuplets' Lullaby
The delightful Dionne Quintuplets appear on cover of this song subtitled "Fifty Chubby Tiny Toes," dedicated to the babies' doctor Allan R. Dafoe. (1935)

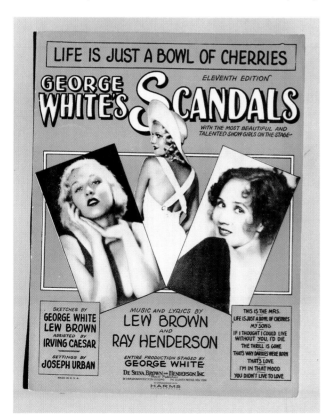

Life Is Just a Bowl of Cherries
Song from *George White's Scandals* by Lew Brown and Ray Henderson preaches, "You work, you save, you worry so, but you can't take your dough when you go, go, go." (1931)

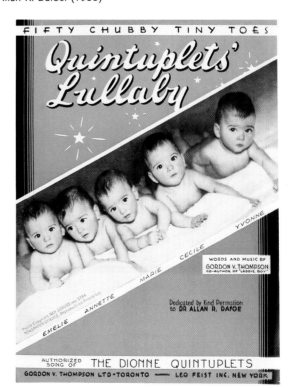

5. Presidents and Politics

Political corruption at the turn of the century did not go unnoticed. The bad reputation of Tammany Hall and the political "bossism" of the Tweed Ring under infamous William Marcy "Boss" Tweed of New York City in the late 1860s continued into the twentieth century. In 1905 Vincent Bryan and Gus Edwards wrote the song "Tammany" described on cover as "a pale face pow-wow" for a gathering of the National Democratic Club of New York. The cover of a leering Indian in feathered headdress belies the actual lyrics of the song which are strongly political in nature. Eight verses good-humoredly poke fun at Tammany and its efforts to clean up its reputation.

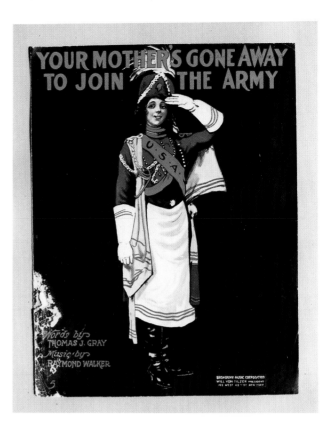

Your Mother's Gone Away to Join the Army
Activist suffragettes sometimes neglected home and family as they marched in parades, campaigning for women's rights. (1913)

Tammany
Song is inscribed to the Honorable Timothy D. Sullivan, and was sung by cover star Jefferson DeAngelis in Sam Shubert's production of *Fantana*. (1905)

The cause of women's suffrage and the right to vote in the United States was pursued with vigor for many years before Congress finally passed the nineteenth amendment to the Constitution in 1920 which mandated, "The right of citizens of the United States to vote shall not be denied or abridged by the United States or by any State on account of sex." As early as 1913 a song was written about mother being absent from home for weeks at a time."She's down at Suffrage Hall...to fight for women's rights."

Taxation has always been a sore subject, not just in the United States, but worldwide. The Stamp Act of 1765 that England imposed on the colonies was one of the reasons for the rebellion that led to the American Revolutionary War. The cost of war is one of a country's major expenses that is financed through taxes. During World War I the War Revenue Act of 1917 raised income taxes to a new high, and imposed a great variety of other taxes that provoked much grumbling throughout the country, and a response in Tin Pan Alley song.

The man in the White House inspired songs all through our country's history—songs about elections, inaugurals, assassinations, and funerals. Presidential sheet music is a prime collectible. The buoyant optimism of the peppy song "Happy Days Are Here Again" was thought by Franklin Roosevelt to reflect his New Deal philosophy in 1932, and it was adopted by the campaign committee as a Democratic theme song and has been used ever since.

Franklin D. Roosevelt March
Roosevelt was well pleased with this William H. Woodin song and inscribed a thank you letter inside the front cover expressing his gratitude, promising to have it played at the inauguration. (1933)

Don't Put a Tax on the Beautiful Girls
The team of Jack Yellen and Milton Ager created a song about taxes that takes a humorous twist, "You can tax my business and all that I own... but leave my pleasure alone!" (1919)

Hello Jimmy
James Earl Carter, 39th president of the United States, held office from 1977 to 1981. (1976)

I Found a Million Dollar Baby
Ronald Reagan, 40th president of the United States, held office from 1981-1989. He starred with Priscilla Lane and Jeffrey Lynn in this Warner Brothers movie before he entered the political arena. (1941)

Happy Days Are Here Again
Cheerful song by Yellen and Ager for the movie *Chasing Rainbows* became the theme song for the Democratic party. (1929)

Unsuccessful running mates in presidential elections also had hopeful campaign songs written for them. Alfred E. Smith, four term Governor of New York state, represented the Democrats against Herbert Hoover in 1928, and had as his official campaign song "The Sidewalks of New York."

The assassination in 1865 of Abraham Lincoln, thought by many to be our country's greatest President, had its parallel in 1963 when President John F. Kennedy was shot down in the streets of Dallas leaving the nation stunned and grief-stricken. In 1968 Robert Kennedy and Martin Luther King Jr. also fell victims to assassination, and Dick Holler composed a touching song in tribute to the fallen heroes.

The Sidewalks of New York
Al Smith, the son of Irish-Catholic immigrants, grew up on the streets of New York. He lost out to Herbert Hoover in the presidential election of 1928.

6. Expositions and Dedications

Collecting exposition, anniversary, and dedication memorabilia is a field in itself. Such music is most often collected for the historical covers, and is of continuing and avid interest, not only to sheet music collectors but also to serious historians. Songs about expositions, world's fairs, dedications, and celebrations of all kinds have been written.

"Seward's Folly" was the name jeeringly given to the purchase of Alaska from Russia for $7,200,000 in 1867. William H. Seward, then Secretary of State, was instrumental in the purchase that soon came to be recognized as a bargain when gold was discovered in the 1880s causing a great gold rush to the Yukon territory.

The wealth and wonder of Alaska was displayed at the Alaska-Yukon-Pacific Exposition in Seattle, Washington, in 1909. Two songs that publicized the exposition were "The Greater Seattle March and Two Step" and "Seattle Exposition March." A comic opera also came out that year, *The Alaskan*, produced by John Cort.

Abraham, Martin and John
"Has anybody here seen my old friend Bobby? I thought I saw him walkin' up over the hill with Abraham, Martin, and John..." (1968)

San Diego, California, the Gem of the U.S.A.
This souvenir song sheet was published as part of the promotion of the Panama-California International Exposition held in San Diego in 1916.

Meet Me in Seattle at the Fair
The Alaskan-Yukon-Pacific Exposition was held on grounds which are now part of the university campus in Seattle. (1909)

For I Dream of You (from The Alaskan)
Romantic song by Theodore H. Northrup from the show *The Alaskan* has attractive lithograph cover by the Strobridge Company featuring two exotic totem poles. (1909)

Songs about Yosemite National Park are of particular interest to California collectors. "I'm Strong for Camp Curry" praised the glories of Yosemite Valley and the beauty of the firefall off Glacier Point which was a nightly tradition at Camp Curry for many years. "The Stentor March" by Maurice Blumenthal is another Camp Curry piece dedicated to David Curry, who was known as the Stentor of the Yosemite for his loud cry that echoed from the top of Glacier Point throughout the valley just before the firefall, "Hello, All's well!"

The completion of the Panama Canal in 1914 was another notable occasion that inspired an outpouring of commemorative songs. "Where the Oceans Meet in Panama" was one such song that reduced the great event to a love song lauding the possibility of a boy in the East and a girl in the West meeting halfway in sunny Panama.

*I'm Strong for Camp Curry
(front cover)*
Now just a memory, the
firefall as it tumbles down
the mountainside is
commemorated on the front
cover. Rare sheet music is
autographed by camp
founder David A. Curry.
(1914)

Let the Fire Fall
Song by Sidney Miller and Carmelita Lopez
praised the beauty of the Yosemite firefall.
The back cover gives the history of a
beautiful and moving tradition that was
phased out as the park became too
crowded. (1952)

I'm Strong for Camp Curry (back cover)
Back cover of "I'm Strong for Camp Curry"
has historic photographs of David Curry
and the original tents, pool, and
auditorium of the complex. (1914)

Where the Oceans Meet in Panama
Cover art by A. W. Loomer shows two ships steaming towards the
opening gates to the canal. (1914)

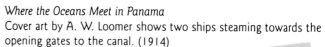

BIBLIOGRAPHY

Books

Barker, Lt. Col. A. J. *Midway*. New York: Galahad Books, 1981.

Bowen, Ezra, Series Editor. *The Fabulous Century*, 5 volumes. New York: Time-Life Books. 1969.

Cornell, James. *The Great International Disaster Book*. New York: Charles Scribner's Sons. 1982.

Current, Richard N., T. Harry Williams, and Frank Freidel. *American History...A Survey*. New York: Alfred A. Knopf, 1961.

Ellis, Edward S. *The History of Our Country*, 9 volumes. Ohio: The Jones Brothers Publishing Company, 1918.

Gammond, Peter. *The Oxford Companion to Popular Music*. New York: Oxford University Press, 1993.

Georgeno, G. N., Editor. *Encyclopedia of American Automobiles*. New York: E. P. Dutton and Company, Inc. 1971.

Jeavons, Clyde. *A Pictorial History of War Films*. New Jersey: The Citadel Press, 1974.

Josephy, Alvin M. Jr., Editor in Charge. *The American Heritage History of Flight*. New York: American Heritage Publishing Company Inc., 1962.

Klamkin, Marian. *Old Sheet Music*. New York: Hawthorn Books Inc., 1975.

Mackey, Frank J. and Marcus Wilson Jernegan. *Forward-March!* Chicago: The Disabled American Veterans of the World War Department of Rehabilitation. 1934-35.

Montgomery, Elizabeth Rider. *The Story Behind Popular Songs*. New York: Cornwall Press, Inc., 1958.

Morison, Samuel Eliot. *The Oxford History of the American People*. New York: Oxford University Press, 1965.

Pater, Alan F. *United States Battleships*. California: Monitor Book Co., 1968.

Pleasants, Henry. *The Great American Popular Singers*. New York: Simon and Schuster, 1974.

Reynolds, Clark G. *War in the Pacific*. New York: Military Press, 1990.

Salomon, Henry. *Victory at Sea*. New York: Doubleday & Company, Inc., 1959.

Simon, George T. *The Big Bands*. Collier-Macmillan Limited, London: The Macmillan Company, 1969.

Swartz, Jon D. and Robert C. Reinehr. *Handbook of Old-Time Radio*. New Jersey: The Scarecrow Press, Inc. 1993.

Terrace, Vincent. *Radio's Golden Years*. California: A. S. Barnes and Company, 1981.

Wallechinsky, David, and Irving Wallace. *The Peoples' Almanac*. New York: Doubleday & Company, Inc., 1975.

Wolfe, Tom. *The Right Stuff*. New York: Bantam Books, 1979.

Periodicals

Life magazine, January 26, 1942. "Casey Jones: Historians Mark His Wreck," pp. 61-67.

Harrington, Clifford V. *The Silent Samurai of the Sea*. Tokyo, Japan: The Information Publishing Ltd., 1963.

Harrity, Sgt. Richard. "G. I. Tunesmith." *Yank, the Army Weekly*, November 16, 1945, 21.

Petruso, Lenore. "Proudly Displaying the Blue Star Flag." *VFW Magazine*, June/July 1991, 18-19.

SONG INDEX AND VALUE GUIDE

Most household or estate music lots found at garage sales, flea markets, and the like are usually common garden variety songs that should retail in the $1-$4 range for most sheets. Topical collectible covers are less often encountered, and values in the $5-$15-$20-plus range are more realistic.

Many variables enter into pricing—rarity, age, demand, historical significance, composer, cover artist, cover personality, and edition. The following value guide is based on a combination of dealers' set price lists, published price guides, auction sales, and the author's own experience. Prices in italics are documented prices known to have been paid at dealers' auctions, which are extremely variable and unpredictable. One can get lucky and pick up a rare piece below market value if the high bidders already have it.

The stated price is for illustrated pieces in *excellent* condition, and should be discounted for lower grades as described in the following condition chart.

Excellent—Very clean, paper still crisp, virtually flawless. May have a music store stamp or a price sticker, as old music store stock was routinely price-stickered in the 1960s and '70s. Full value.

Good—Piece in nice shape, desirable for a collection with no immediate need to upgrade. May show some wear—small tears (less than 3/4"), careful taped repair on inside, inconspicuous signature, store stamp, or price sticker on cover 25% discount.

Fair—Considerable wear from use, and one or more problems like light soil, creases, tears, frayed edges, separated cover, prominent signatures, stickers, or name stamps. 50% discount.

Poor—Complete, but with one or more mutilation problems, such as ragged edges with large tears or pieces missing, folds and/or creases, heavy soiling, sloppy taped repairs, bold writing or doodling, trimmed down from large size. Generally too worn to be of collectible value, unless rare and in a major collectible category 90% discount.

Song Title	Value	Page
Abraham, Martin, and John	$5	170
Adolph	$12	127
Airplane Flight, The	$6	54
Airport 1975	$5	58
Airship Parade, The	$10	48
All Alone	$4	12
Aloha, Soldier Boy	$3-5	118
Am I Wasting My Time on You	$3	15
Amelia Earhart's Last Flight	$15-20 ($47)	54
America First	$8	120
America, Here's My Boy	$5	97
America, He's for You!	$8	98
Anchors Aweigh (Roosevelt)	$10	135
And Russia Is Her Name	$7	149
Anne and Lindy	$25	160
Another Little Dream Won't Do Us Any Harm	$50	56
Answer Mr. Wilson's Call	$11 ($15)	96
Any Bonds Today?	$4	131
Are We Downhearted? No! No! No!	$8	115
Arms for the Love of America	$7	130
Army Air Corps Song, The	$2 ($10)	131
Around the World	$5	42
As the *Lusitania* Went Down	$10	95
As Time Goes By	$15	141
At Mail Call Today	$5 ($10)	145
Au Revoir, but Not Goodbye	$3-5	117
Back Home	$15	54
Back in the Old Town Tonight	$8	114
Band Played "Nearer My God to Thee", The	$15	155
Bang the Bell Rang	$10	55
Bartender Bill	$5	165
Battle in the Sky	$20	45
Battle of Gettysburg, The	$30	7, 77
Battle of Manila March and Two-Step	$8	82
Battle of the Nations	$20 ($29)	73
Be a Hero, My Boy	$10	127
Beautiful Isle of Somewhere	$10	80
Belgium, Dry Your Tears	$8	95
Bell Bottom Trousers	$2	150
Berlin Special, The	$8 ($15)	120
Big Boy Jess	$12	55
Bingity, Bangity, Boom! Boom, Boom!	$6	60
Blaze Away	$8	82
Bless 'Em All (Cagney)	$8	57
Blue and the Gray, The	$8	83
Bombardier Song, The	$6	136
Boy and a Girl Were Dancing, A (Etting)	$5	26
Boys in Blue Are Turning Gray, The	$8	79
Break the News to Mother (Span-Am)	$8	85
Brother, Can You Spare a Dime? (from show *Americana*)	$6	167
Burning of Rome, The	$12 ($20)	153
Burning Iroquois, The	$12-15	158
Buy a Bond Today	$7	132
By the Fireside	$2	19
Byrd, You're the Bird of Them All	$20	54
Cable Car Song, The	$15	39
Caissons Go Rolling Along, The	$4	136
Call for Mr Brown	$8	14
Canteen Bounce, The	$4	141
Captain of Industry (from movie *Tucker*)	$7	67
Carry Me Off in a Big Balloon	$15	43
Casey Jones	$15	35
Casey Jones Went Down on the Robert E. Lee	$8	36
Charge of the Roosevelt Rough Riders, The	$12	87
Chattanooga Choo Choo	$6	41
Chauffeur, The	$25	62
Check and Double Check	$15	22
Chicago Express, The	$15	29
Children of the Battle Field, The	$50	78
Ciribiribin	$8	25
Civilization Peace Song	$10	94
Cleanin' My Rifle (and Dreamin' of You)	$5 ($10)	147
Cloud Kisser	$15 ($22)	47
Come Fly With Me	$5	55
Come Josephine in My Flying Machine	$8 ($20)	47
Come on Love, Say Hello	$8	12
Come Take a Trip in My Airship	$13	43
Comet, The	$12	60
Comin' in on a Wing and a Prayer	$2	144
Commander-in-Chief	$5	119
Cradle Song	$4	24
Cuba Liberty March	$30	83
Dapper Dan	$5	32
Daytime, Nighttime and You	$3	23
Defend Your Country	$13	127
Der Fuehrer's Face	$25	151
Dig Her Deep in Dixie	$12	90
Dixie Volunteers, The	$5	99
Does This Railroad Lead to Heaven?	$8	36
Don't Bite the Hand that's Feeding You	$5	96
Don't Put a Tax on the Beautiful Girls	$5	169
Don't Sit Under the Apple Tree (G. Miller)	$5 ($12)	150
Don't Take My Darling Boy Away	$6	92
Don't Talk	$12	128
Down Where the Wurzburger Flows	$5	163
Dream in My Heart, The (Sinatra, H. James)	$7	23
Drummer Boy of '76, The	$8	74
Each Stitch Is a Thought of You, Dear	$6	99
Empire Express	$20	30
Every Boy's a Hero in This War Today	$5	120
Every Day of My Life	$5	26
Everybody's Happy Now	$5	125
Ev'rybody Ev'ry Payday	$7 ($14)	132
Father of the Land We Love	$8	75
Fighting Navy (of the Good Old U.S.A.), The	$8	110
Fighting Quartermaster Corps, The	$10 ($15)	134
Find the Lindbergh Baby, Most Wanted in the Land	$50	160
Flight of the Aeronauts, The	$10	43
Flight of the Air Ship	$20	44
For I Dream of You (from *The Alaskan*)	$5	171
For the Sake of Wife and Home	$8 ($12)	161
For Your Boy and My Boy	$3-5	122
Forty-Five Minutes from Broadway	$8	109
Franklin D. Roosevelt March	$10	169
Freedom Train	$6	38
Fuehrer's Swan Song, The	$30	148
G.I. Jive	$3	150
Gasoline Gus and His Jitney Bus	$16 ($20)	64
Gem O' My Heart	$4	19
General Grant's Funeral March	$25	79
General Pershing's Grand March	$12	116
Girl in White, The	$8	34